THE MISS TUTTI FRUTTI CONTEST

ALSO BY GRAEME LAY

TRAVEL

Passages: Journeys in Polynesia

Pacific New Zealand

The Cook Islands (with Ewan Smith)

New Zealand – A Visual Celebration (with Gareth Eyres)

Samoa (with Evotia Tamua)

Feasts & Festivals (with Glenn Jowitt)

The Globetrotter Guide to New Zealand

Are We There Yet? A Kiwi Kid's Holiday Exploring Guide

The Best of Auckland

NOVELS AND SHORT STORY COLLECTIONS

The Mentor

The Fools on the Hill

Temptation Island

Dear Mr Cairney

Motu Tapu: Stories of the South Pacific

The Town on the Edge of the World

YOUNG ADULT NOVELS

The Wave Rider

Leaving One Foot Island

Return to One Foot Island

The Pearl of One Foot Island

EDITOR

Metro Fiction

100 New Zealand Short Short Stories

Another 100 New Zealand Short Short Stories

The Third Century

Boys' Own Stories

50 Short Short Stories by Young New Zealanders

An Affair of the Heart: A Celebration of Frank Sargeson's Centenary
(with Stephen Stratford)

Golden Weather: North Shore Writers Past & Present
(with Jack Ross)

THE MISS TUTTI FRUTTI CONTEST
TRAVEL TALES OF THE SOUTH PACIFIC
GRAEME LAY

AWA PRESS

Published in 2004 by Awa Press, PO Box 11-416, Wellington, New Zealand

© Graeme Lay 2004

National Library of New Zealand Cataloguing-in-Publication Data
Lay, Graeme, 1944-
The Miss Tutti Frutti contest: travel tales of the South Pacific
by Graeme Lay
ISBN 0-9582509-0-1
1. Lay, Graeme, 1944—Travel—Polynesia. 2. Polynesia—
Description and travel.
919.604—dc 22

The author and publisher would like to acknowledge those publications in which some material
originally appeared: Tandem Press for some of the Niue, Tonga and Rarotonga material in
Passages: Journeys in Polynesia, and the journey into the heart of Tahiti in their anthology
A Passion for Travel; Metro for first publishing the story of the visit to the
Outer Islands of the Cook Group and a version of the Tonga story; the New Zealand Listener
for Herman Melville's story and the hike on Tahiti Iti; North & South for the 'Losing Errol' story;
Canvas for the Gauguin story and 'The Miss Tutti Frutti Contest', and Cuisine for a version of
story of the Hawaiiki Nui Va'a. Acknowledgement is also made to the estates of the writers
Herman Melville, H.E. Bates and Robert Louis Stevenson for the incorporation
of some of these writers' lines in the text.

Cover illustration 'Lagoon' by Andy Leleisi'uao
Author photograph by Jane Ussher
Map by Geographx

Designed by Sarah Maxey, Wellington
Typeset by Jill Livestre, Archetype, Wellington
Printed by Astra Print, Wellington

www.awapress.com

In memory of my father
Donald Luigi Lay (1914–97)
who served with the New Zealand Army
in the South Pacific in World War Two

CONTENTS

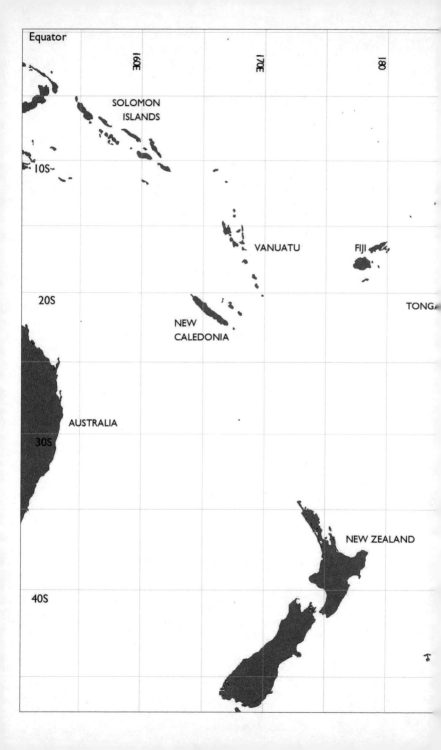

MARQUESAS
ISLANDS •

SAMOA

LEEWARD
ISLANDS •

•• TUAMOTU ISLANDS
SOCIETY ISLANDS
(TAHITI)

• NIUE

COOK •
ISLANDS

SOUTH PACIFIC

INTRODUCTION

OUNTLESS THOUSANDS of international travellers have seen the Pacific – through the windows of a jet liner cruising at 11,000 metres. Far fewer have seen it at sea level, or visited some of the scores of high islands and atolls which are strewn across Earth's largest ocean like constellations in a watery universe. Just to fly over this universe is to miss a great deal, for each of the inhabited islands of the Pacific is a miniature world, with its own distinctive culture and way of life. *The Miss Tutti Frutti Contest* is about my exploration of some of these island worlds and my encounters with some of their inhabitants.

My fascination with islands began long before I ever went to one. As a boy growing up in a small town on the rocky, windswept Taranaki coast, the sea became an intimate part of my life. Rock-pool exploration, fishing, swimming, surfing: all these activities brought me into close contact with the sea. And as an avid reader from early boyhood, the books I read – sea adventure stories, mainly – reflected this intimacy. If the story was set on an island, I found it irresistible. I remember in particular reading and re-reading my father's copy of *The Coral Island*, by R. M. Ballantyne, along with Robert Louis Stevenson's *Treasure Island* and Enid Blyton's *Five on a Treasure Island*. In my imagination, islands were places of romance and adventure, exotic locations with infinite possibilities.

When I first visited the islands of the South Pacific as an adult twenty years ago, I was in no way disappointed by what I found there. The islands' shores, reefs, lagoons and forests captivated me. From their coasts or mountains the Pacific Ocean's beauty and changing moods could be readily observed: silken and docile one day, tempestuous and threatening the next. And every day, spellbinding.

Added to these natural attractions were the people I encountered, the locals as well as the often bizarre outsiders who had made the Pacific their adopted home. The indigenous cultures reached back into the sea mists of prehistory. There were languages which had been spoken for thousands of years, songs, dances and art which traced their history, and whose appeal was alluring. Superimposed on these traditional cultures was the introduced way of life of the Europeans and Asians – men mainly – who had come to the South Pacific for a variety of reasons, some honourable, some not. The subsequent blending of these cultures and peoples has produced something unique and special in the islands of the South Pacific.

The stories in this book are the collected accounts of many separate journeys taken over the last decade, at times conflated to iron out the creases. They are intended primarily to entertain, but if readers become informed as well, that will be gratifying. The collection confines itself to the islands of tropical Polynesia – rather than the other great Pacific cultural spheres of Melanesia and Micronesia – because it is in Polynesia that this writer's interest lies. It is not intended to be a guidebook; there are many of those already available. Instead, it tries to convey some of the enchantment and surprise I have found when visiting the islands of the South Pacific – islands best savoured not from high in the the air, but with feet firmly on the ground or dipped in the warm ocean waters.

GRAEME LAY
July 2004

ONE

ME AND MY TUMUNU
NGAPUTORU,
COOK ISLANDS

IN COOK ISLANDS MAORI they're called Ngaputoru, the Three Roots. Atiu, Mitiaro and Mauke are a trio of raised, flat-topped coral atolls, forty minutes by air north-east of Rarotonga. For years they've teased my curiosity whenever I've spied them on a map; now at last I'm on my way to see them.

It's hard to stay aloof from your fellow passengers when there are eighteen of you in a twenty-seater plane. The seating configuration lends itself to instant intimacy. Right alongside me are a German couple in their late twenties. He is small and compact, with black hair already flecked with grey; she has short brown hair, green eyes, moulded cheekbones and a permanently wide-eyed expression. Both have tanned, olive skin. Jurgen and Helga are thoroughly natty. Their clothing is chic-casual; they look like models from some de luxe department store in their home city of Cologne. Helga carries a video camera which she claps to her right eye socket and points at the mountains of Rarotonga as we soar from the island's runway. Then they laugh and chatter excitedly for a time, before Jurgen puts his head on her shoulder and dozes off.

Behind me is an Australian family of four: Deidre and Gavin and their two small boys, Troy and Zane. Troy, who at six is the elder by a year, is the strong, silent type; Zane speaks for both boys, loudly: 'Hey! Wow! Look! The propeller's goin' *fast!* Look, Mum, look at how eet's goin'. Hey, Dad! We're mooveen, we're mooven!'

Gavin's short and stocky, with long, crinkly blond hair and a flushed face. He wears a red T-shirt that proclaims that Tooheys is Simply The Best. Deidre turns to me and introduces herself. She's small and clear-skinned and must have been pretty once, but now she's hollow-chested and her long brown hair's gone dead at the ends. They run a pub in upstate Victoria. No wonder Deidre looks tired: it must be hard being a publican's wife in Wobbadonga. They've come to the Cook Islands, Gavin explains, to make a complete break and to show the boys the sea. 'We've got another one at home,' says Deidre, looking even wearier at the thought. 'Three months old. He's staying with Gavin's folks.' She sighs philosophically, wipes Zane's streaming nose, gives me a rueful smile. 'Three boys under seven ...'

As I stare through the windshield between the two Air Rarotonga pilots, a level, green, reef-ringed island comes into sight. Mitiaro. The plane begins to descend, swaying and dipping towards a white crushed-coral runway.

Neither I nor the Aussie family are getting off here – we're on our way to Atiu – but Jurgen and Helga are. The plane taxis towards the terminal, a blue and yellow fibrolite shed in front of a stand of coconut palms. As it comes to a shuddering halt, we can see that something important is happening.

The front porch of the shed is crammed with people. Six very fat, barefoot women are leaping, singing and wriggling their hips to the accompaniment of another two women who are thumping bass drums. Helga points her video camera at the window and presses the trigger.

The plane door opens and we disembark. The crowd in the terminal rushes towards us. They are almost all women, all large, all singing at the tops of their voices and wriggling their hips in a none too subtle mime. They are covered in thick garlands of fern, flowers and pandanus leaves. Two of the women, who are so festooned with foliage they look like matching Christmas trees, come aboard the plane. They are weeping – the party is evidently their farewell.

There's no apparent sadness on the part of the others, though. They simply redirect their emotions towards the German couple, who are quickly surrounded by the shouting, cackling band. The drums are thumped even more vigorously as Jurgen and Helga are borne away to the rear of the terminal building and a rusting Bedford truck which looks as if it should be an exhibit in a transport museum. The Germans' Gucci luggage is tossed aboard and pandanus leis are thrust over their heads as they're bundled on to the tray of the truck.

The rest of us are now back on the plane, watching the welcoming show through the windows. Jurgen and Helga are completely engulfed; we can just see their two faces, fixed in a rictus of astonishment and apprehension, as the truck moves off along a dusty road.

I'm staying in a chalet near the top of the central dome of Atiu. The view reminds me of East Africa, which is odd because I've never been to East Africa. Perhaps I'm remembering pictures I've seen of the Kenyan highlands. Below me are stands of spreading acacia trees; to my left the land falls away steeply to a sweep of rain-forest canopy; and in the foreground are patches of bare, henna-coloured earth and clumps of banana palms.

Unlike almost any other South Pacific island, nearly all the action on Atiu takes place up here, on the plateau. Here on the dome are the island's five seemingly contiguous village houses, and its shops, churches and schools. As with most raised atolls, this one is surrounded by a crown of thorns, a ring of wickedly sharp, fossilised coral known in the Cook Islands as makatea. But the land immediately behind the coastal makatea looks fertile enough, so why does everyone on Atiu live as far as it's possible to get from the sea, the reef, the fishing grounds and the canoe landings? Because the missionaries decreed it.

In the old days the Atiuans were the Vikings of these islands, regularly setting off in their canoes to plunder their neighbours. One of the most feared of their leaders was the warrior chief Rongomatane, who led his men on several conquering raids of Mitiaro and Mauke. Then in 1823 a zealous missionary, John Williams, arrived on Atiu. Rongo-matane quickly became one of Williams' converts and ordered the destruction of the Atiuans' traditional deities. And where Rongomatane went the others had to follow. Almost over-night, Atiu and the other two Roots turned Christian. John Williams, meanwhile, went on to successfully introduce the new faith into Samoa but conspicuously failed to do so when he arrived in the New Hebrides – now Vanuatu – in 1839. There, on the island of Erromango, he was clubbed to death and eaten.

On Atiu the gospel merchants – working, possibly, on a rough-and-ready 'Nearer My God to Thee' principle – had their churches built way up on the central dome, and the people followed. The big white Cook Islands Christian Church – Ziona Tapu – is certainly imposing, and there's a logic in centralising settlement, but even a quick look at the island has convinced me that if I were an Atiuan I would prefer to live by the sea.

Gavin and Deidre have hired mopeds to take themselves and the boys around the island, but I'm suspicious of those seemingly innocuous vehicles, especially on Atiu's unsealed roads. I prefer a push-bike, and I've managed to borrow one. It's a women's model, old, with brakes that squeal like a pig being slaughtered, but otherwise serviceable.

Coming down off the dome on my bike, freewheeling through the dense forest to the makatea zone, is an exhila-rating experience, tempered by the certainty that at some stage I'll have to push the bike back up again. Brakes shrieking, I career down a winding, rutted road to the coastal plain on the island's western side. Here the huge trees meet to form a tunnel of tropical foliage. It's cool and utterly silent, and I haven't seen or heard another human so far. But, foolishly, I didn't bring a water bottle, and it's tiring pushing this gearless bike along what is just a sandy track. Out on the coast I stop to inspect the white-sand beaches of Tumai and Taungaroro, which are incised into the mostly rocky coast. Little coves enclosed on three sides by grey fossilised coral, they're deserted and undeniably beautiful, but the sun is high in the brilliant blue sky and I'm close to being dehydrated.

I remount, bike on through the forest, where it is at least cool, and pass the place where Captain James Cook and his crew came ashore in April 1777 in search of feed for the cattle on board the *Resolution*. He got instead bananas, a pig and some coconuts, giving in exchange a bolt of cloth and a small axe. Usually I can't resist visiting a Cook landing place, but now other urges take precedence. I keep on pedalling, heading along the coast in search of drinkable fluid. My legs ache and I'm saddle-sore. My pedalling pace grows slower, my thighs sorer, my mouth drier. Somewhere up ahead there *must* be a shop, or at least a house. If there isn't, I will collapse.

The forest parts, the road forks. Checking my map, I see that I'm at Taunganui harbour, where Atiu's imports are barge-loaded from small cargo ships and brought ashore. A couple of Atiuans are sitting on a beached barge, chipping with no enthusiasm at its surface rust, while a group of men repose in the big, open-sided cargo shed at the top of a slip. I dump the bike and stagger up to the shed.

'Kia orana. Is there a shop round here?'

A tall, powerfully built man in shorts shakes his head. 'Only shop up in the village.'

It's back on the plateau. I'll never make it.

The men are looking at me curiously. I must look like someone who's stumbled out of the Gobi Desert.

'What you want?' asks the tall man.

'A drink. I'm … very thirsty.'

He walks over to a crate, on top of which are half a dozen husked coconuts. He cracks the top of one deftly with a machete, as if it's a boiled egg, flips off its lid and passes it over. I swig at its opening until the sweet juice overflows from my mouth and runs down my chin. It's fresh, pure, reviving, and I wonder, is there a finer drink in all the world than this? Not for the first time, I have been saved by a coconut.

The only light is a low flame from a rag wick sticking out of the top of a small tin filled with diesel. The makeshift lamp sits on a crate and only partially illuminates the faces of my six companions. We are sitting on wooden benches around the crate in a kikau-thatched, earth-floored hut, surrounded by forest and the blackness of the tropical night. One of the men says a prayer, then lifts the banana-palm leaf which covers the container at his feet. Dipping a small coconut-shell cup into the container, he passes it to the man on his right.

The man drinks, passes the cup back. The leaf is removed again, the cup filled, then passed to the next man. He drinks, passes it back. Curiously, expectantly, I await my turn. I am at the end of the circle. The cup is dipped, passed to me. I swig its contents. The drink is flat, fruity, with a taste of earth. I nod approvingly, and pass it back to the head, who says solemnly, 'So, Graeme, kia orana. Welcome to the Matavai tumunu.'

Tumunu literally means the hollowed-out base of that most versatile of trees, the coconut palm. It makes a fine container for any liquid, but particularly bush-brewed beer. Tumunu has thus come to mean the place where men gather to consume the beer, a place deep in the forest. Atiu has several tumunu and visitors are welcome, provided they observe the protocol.

When the missionaries proscribed the consumption of alcohol in the late nineteenth century, the Atiuans, along with the other Cook Islanders who had developed a liking for liquor, were obliged to find furtive methods of producing it. As the missionaries had also brought hundreds of orange trees to the island, Tahitian visitors taught their Atiuan cousins the art of brewing 'beer' using the citrus fruit as a base, with sugar, yeast and malt added to assist in a speedy and potent fermentation process. The 'bush beer' took only a few days to make and, as its consumption was necessarily a clandestine business, the tumunu were sited within the forest, far from the prying eyes of the London Missionary Society wowsers.

Today the tumunu are legal (although the last conviction for public drunkenness resulting from a tumunu session was recorded as recently as 1987) and attended two or three times a week. The most popular session is, apparently, after Sunday morning worship.

The cup continues to circulate. Each man makes a speech about himself and his thoughts on anything he considers worth airing. One man, who is indistinct in the gloom but appears to be in his fifties, is incapable of completing a sentence. Each time, he starts by saying something like, 'To me, I feel that the important thing is that we make a chance to ...' Then he fades into incoherence, and the cup is passed on.

After a few more rounds and a few more speeches, I realise that all my companions are drunk. In fact when I think back to the beginning of the session (now not so easy to do), I realise they were drunk when I arrived. The latest rounds were just topping them up. I have been warned that the bush-brew is ferociously potent, so I begin to 'pass' every other round, holding up my hand in a 'halt' gesture when the cup is passed to me. My friends, though, don't miss a drink. Round and round the cup goes, on and on goes the talk. Voices are now *very* slurred, all utterances difficult to follow. The older man's sentences are further truncated: 'I think ... to me ... I feel ... that the important thing ...' His hands shake, his voice fails him, his cup, as it were, runneth over.

Knowing that I must leave if I am to find my way back to the chalet in the darkness, I am nevertheless reluctant. I have a feeling of intense euphoria, of comradeship towards the tumunu, towards *my* tumunu, and towards my new Atiuan mates. We all make farewell speeches and I dredge up my few phrases of Cook Islands Maori. We shake hands solemnly and sorrowfully. The leader declares, slurringly, 'Graeme, you must not get lost on your way back. Nga will guide you through the forest and back to the road.' Nga is the man whose sentences cannot be brought to a coherent conclusion.

Nga takes me by the hand and leads me through the black forest. His physical skills are much better than his verbal ones, and in minutes we're out of the trees and on the road.

There he claps his hand on my shoulder and at last finishes a sentence: 'I hear … you say … you have a daughter. In her twenties. I must tell you … I have no wife … no children. So I would also like to say … that I offer myself … to marry … your daughter.'

I politely decline this proposal on my daughter Rebecca's behalf and, after shaking hands again, walk off down the road. 'Take … the … left fork …' Nga has instructed. Carefully.

I've been told that bush beer paralyses the legs, but mine feel okay. My head's clear too, very clear, and I still have an overwhelming feeling of goodwill towards my tumunu companions. Overhead the sky is crammed with stars, their light so clear and strong they shimmer and pulsate, appearing to rush down and engulf me as I trip on through the blackness in the direction of my motel.

Next night I dine with the local priest, Father Johann, who has lived on Atiu for many years. When I mention the tumunu his face turns overcast. 'The tumunu,' he pronounces in his still-thick Friesland accent, 'cause more trouble than anything else.' I press him for details, which he quickly supplies. Bush beer is addictive and fiercely alcoholic. It causes mental deterioration and endless social problems. Regular drinkers of bush beer rarely see sixty.

Somewhat defensively, I tell the priest that I enjoyed the camaraderie of the tumunu, and the talk. His expression now turns hostile. 'What exactly did you talk about with them?' he demands. I summarise the session.

As I do so he nods reproachfully. Everything, but *everything* my tumunu friends told me was lies. The Atiu traditional sailing canoe *wasn't* the only one that made it unassisted to Rarotonga last year from the Outer Islands; Cook Islanders *didn't* have alcohol before the papa'a (Europeans) introduced it; the local MP *hasn't* done much for this island, and so on.

This is all a bit sobering, especially since Father Johann is no wowser – he and I are drinking wine, a mead-type brew he has made himself from honey. So, to leaven the conversation, I add, 'One of the men who doesn't have a wife proposed marriage to my daughter. That was an interesting gesture.'

The priest looks at me sharply. 'Which man was that?'

'Nga. Chap of about fifty-five. Skinny bloke.'

Father Johann's expression becomes one of disgust. 'Nga Taputa. He has a wife all right. And nine children.'

Later, back on Rarotonga, a local construction contractor tells me about a big concreting job that needed doing on Atiu. He agreed to hire out his ready-mixed concrete truck to the Atiuans, and it was shipped over to the island. Weeks passed, he needed the concrete truck back, but every time he called Atiu he was told the weather was too rough and it couldn't be loaded for the return voyage. Finally he became impatient, checked on the weather and was told that it was perfect, that the sea off Atiu was dead calm. He flew over to retrieve his vehicle. He found it in spotless condition, cleaner than he had ever known it to be. It was so clean because no concrete had passed through its bowl. The locals were finding it the perfect receptacle for mixing huge batches of bush beer, with the additional advantage of portability.

On my last night on Atiu, Gavin and Deidre ask me over

to their bungalow for a beer. As Zane and Troy explore the pineapple patch next door, Gavin pours me a can of Tooheys.

'Where did you get this?' I ask him curiously. I haven't seen anything but Steinlager on Atiu.

'Brought a few trays over with us. That's the best part about bringin' the boys. We used most of their baggage allowance up in Tooheys.'

I tell them about the bush beer session. Gavin's immediately very keen to go to a tumunu. 'What do you feel like when you drink it?' asks Deidre, eyeing Gavin uneasily.

'Very peaceful, very friendly. Not at all aggressive.'

'More like an aphrodeesiac?' she suggests.

Gavin gives her a sharp glance. 'No, no, it can't be that,' he says.

Deidre frowns as she sips her Tooheys. 'Oh no, not an aphrodeesiac – that's not the word I'm lookin' for. What's the word for what you were describing?'

'A sedative?' I suggest. The brew had had a sleep-inducing effect.

Deidre shakes her head. 'No, no, not a sedateeve. I mean a word that makes you, you know, feel like going to sleep.'

There's an avian curiosity on Atiu, a type of swift called the kopeka, which lives in one of the island's many caves. The cave is called Anatakitaki, and it's reached after a half-hour walk through the forest and across the makatea. Keen to visit it, I join a small team the next day – a middle-aged American bird-watching couple, Kelvin and Gloria, who look like stilts, pale and tall with long thin legs; a local guide called Tereapii;

and a shy teenage boy called Junior. We tramp through the forest, its floor made of the flint-hard fossilised coral, until we come to a deep, jagged-edged hole. We leave our day-packs and other belongings beside the pit, then scramble down with the aid of a rope. Carefully Tereapii and Junior guide us into the hole, then Junior, his contribution made, heads back home. The rest of us are led by Tereapii through various rock formations and eventually to the track that leads to the mouth of Anatakitaki cave.

It's a vast chamber containing beautifully fluted, alabaster-like columns of calcite. On one side the chamber is open to the sky, with tropical sunlight streaming down on the columns, while on the other it descends to a series of caverns complete with stalactites and stalagmites. We take a short walk into the cave. Tereapii waves a torch and the little kopekas dart around the roof and walls, making a distinctive clicking sound, like a Geiger counter over pay dirt. The kopekas flit and click as they make their way to and from their nests, located on small ledges near the roof.

Outside the cave, the kopekas never rest. They swoop about non-stop, catching insects on the wing, then bringing them back to the cave to feed to their nestlings. As the birds do not click beyond the cave, ornithologists theorise that the noise is an echo-sounding device, a type of radar which allows them to find their way about in the darkness of the chamber. After a tentative exploration of the cave, I leave Tereapii, Kelvin and Gloria to it, and return to the head of the track. I need to buy some of Atiu's excellent coffee in the village before leaving the island.

The next day, Gloria and Kelvin are at the airport waiting for the same plane, and as soon as I see them I can tell that something has gone seriously wrong. Kelvin is visibly furious, his thin face tightly drawn as he paces about and glances at his watch. Gloria looks as if she has been crying. What on earth can have happened, on this sleepy island? Then a car draws up and Tereapii gets out. She approaches the bird-watching couple, wringing her hands, her expression distraught. 'I am *so* sorry,' she says, over and over. The couple turn away, obviously still fuming. Did they not see enough kopekas or something? After asking some discreet questions of the man whose chalet I've been renting and who's also at the airport, I find out.

It was Junior. After turning back from the trek, he rifled the American's bags and stole a sum of money. Kelvin and Gloria discovered the theft last night and contacted Tereapii, who confronted Junior, who confessed. Tereapii then went to see his family, and the money – 150 dollars – was retrieved. The Americans felt violated; they had been told the island was without crime. Watching them now, barely able to wait until they take off, I can see that a terrible betrayal has occurred – not the sum of money so much as a loss of innocence. When they think of this island they won't remember the kopeka, or the coffee, or the dignity of the Ziona Tapu church. They will remember only that they were robbed. As for Junior, my host told me, 'He'll get a beating he'll never forget.' Watching the stony-faced Americans as we wait for the plane to take off, I have a sinking feeling in my stomach. Sometimes the inequalities exposed by tourism do nobody any good.

The Three Roots are similar in shape (lozenge-like) and size (about fifteen kilometres in circumference). But these geographical similarities are misleading; all are distinctive in at least one respect. The first thing I notice after arriving on Mitiaro is that its villages are where they should be, beside the sea and on the western or leeward side of the island. There are three villages, scattered around Omutu landing, and they're all sleepy, pretty and sheltered, bisected by a wide sandy avenue lined with tall Norfolk pines and flame trees. Their verandahed houses and the big Cook Islands Christian Church are well spaced and surrounded by expanses of grass. On the verandahs women sit chatting, weaving pandanus mats or making clothes on antique sewing machines.

I'm transferred to my accommodation by the same old truck which met Jurgen and Helga. The driver drops off air freight at houses along the way to Nane Pokoati's guest-house. There are just six tourist beds on Mitiaro, and they're all at Nane's.

Nane is in her early forties, short, plump, frizzy-haired, and with a round face that's laughing more often than not. Her house is just a pawpaw's toss from Omutu landing. It's big and airy, with low ceilings and wide porches at the front and rear: the sort of house I'm in for five minutes and feel right at home. Nane's elderly mother, who speaks no English, lives here too, while her late husband sleeps peacefully in a big grave in the front garden.

I sink down on to a sofa on the back porch, screened from the afternoon sun by a curtain of beige pandanus leaves, and Nane brings me a plate of poke – mashed, baked bananas. As

I eat the thick, filling pudding, I look out over the back yard. On the washing line, neatly pegged, are two big blue towels, two snorkels, two pairs of flippers, and two day-glo orange pairs of diving gloves. Designer diving equipment.

'You have other guests, Nane?'

'Yes, two.'

'Are they from Germany?'

'Yes. How did you know?'

'I just guessed. Where are they now?'

'They have gone for a walk. All the time, they walk, these people.'

There are others, not tourists, staying at Nane's: three of her young nieces – Kura, Krissie and Kristine. Kristine, who's never been to Mitiaro before, is the most gorgeous of a trio of beautiful girls. Her skin is as smooth and pale as coconut cream, her hair thick and black, her eyelashes lustrous and long. Everyone, male and female, falls in love with Kristine. And what intensifies our passion is that she seems completely unaware of the effect she has on us. Mostly she sleeps, sprawled out on the double bed on the back porch, and when she wakes she always falls into someone's arms.

Kristine is three weeks old.

And it is the old lady – Mama – who dotes on Kristine more than anyone else. The baby lies in her lap, sleeping, or gazing up with unblinking eyes into her kindly, wrinkled face.

In mid-afternoon, two perspiring figures come around the corner of the house. Jurgen and Helga have been for a walk across the island. Still wearing their Euro-designer gear, they're sweating under their natty shorts and Italian sports shoes, and gratefully accept the glasses of freshly squeezed lime juice that Nane pours them. (Mitiaro grows superb limes.) The three of us catch up on our movements since we were last together on the plane.

'Did you see what happened to us when we arrived at z'airport?' asks Jurgen.

'I did, yes.'

He shakes his head in disbelief. 'That was … the most amazing welcome. All that singing … and dancing …'

Helga, bright-eyed, chips in. 'I was so excited, I forget, mmm, I for*got*, to video this welcome. Now, when I tell people in Chermany about it, they do not … they should not … they *will* not believe me, I don't think.'

We all laugh again at the memory of their riotous induction into Mitiaro society. But I still can't help thinking how incongruous the couple seem here. They look like Riviera, not Mitiaro people. I ask them, 'And now you've seen the island, what do you think of it?'

Their faces become radiant. Helga gushes: 'Oh, we love it here.' Jurgen nods wildly in agreement.

'But … what do you do?'

Jurgen looks thoughtful. 'We walk, and we snorkel, and we look for beaches around the edge of the island. Every day we are doing this.'

Helga tells me they have found deep pools in the reef which have the clearest water and the most beautiful fish they've ever seen. At low tide they spend hours snorkelling there and photographing the fish with their underwater cameras.

I warm to Jurgen and Helga, who are genial, sensitive, tolerant people. Back in Cologne they live a life of affluence, sophistication and industriousness for eleven months of the year, then for the other month they fly across the world to the South Pacific and seek out an isolated tropical island like Mitiaro, where they can do ... nothing. No movies, no restaurants or cafes, no nightclubs, no shops. And no crowds, no acid rain, no mines, no neo-Nazis, no autobahns. Helga and Jurgen are so green they're almost fluorescent.

Each of the Three Roots can lay claim to a unique natural feature. Mitiaro has a lake, something of a rarity in this part of the world. Strictly speaking, there're two linked lakes, called Rotoiti and Rotonui, and they lie near the eastern edge of the island, surrounded by the forbidding, scalpel-sharp rocks of the makatea.

Nane, Jurgen, Helga and I are driven down a rough track to the shore of Rotonui on the back of the all-purpose Bedford. The lake is a bleak sight, black and sedgy at the margins, the water sullen and still, the sort of lake from which you could easily imagine a chain-mailed arm emerging to receive Excalibur. But what comes from this lake is not an armoured arm but eels, known locally as itiki.

As with all eels, there is an element of mystery attached to the itiki's comings and goings. They probably slither a kilometre through the makatea from the sea, then live in the lake until they're about a metre long. They're prized throughout the Cook Islands – the equivalent of caviar. That evening Nane cooks some itiki for dinner. Its black skin and face are almost repulsive, but the flesh is very pink, sweet and flavoursome.

Now we drive to the eastern side of Mitiaro, bouncing along on the tray of the truck. It's unpopulated here, blasted by the south-easterly trade winds, a landscape of jagged grey coral where only small spiky pandanus plants grow. But the road is being re-formed, and there are piles of white sand which will be its new foundation. Nane intends to make a complete circuit of the island, but about three-quarters of the way round the dial the route is blocked by a big heap of sand and an ancient grader. There's no way through, so the driver reverses the Bedford, turns it round and we return the way we came. The wind whips our hair into weird styles, but Nane is still laughing, Jurgen still looks entranced and Helga is still smiling, turning her face gratefully towards the setting sun.

'The only thing wrong with Mitiaro,' sighs Jurgen, 'is that there is no beer.'

It's true, there's not a full can or bottle on the island until the supply boat arrives next week from Rarotonga. This is dismaying news for beer drinkers like Jurgen and me. However, by the merest chance I have a large bottle of duty-free brandy in my bag, and there are appreciative looks all round when I produce it before dinner. Mixed with Mitiaro lime juice, and drunk with our de facto extended family on Nane's back porch, it draws us even closer together.

Next day I go for a walk along the wide, straight, sandy street that passes through the villages. The sun is high, the day is windless, the children are in school, and Mitiaro seems deserted, apart from me and the dogs.

In the Cook Islands there are islands with dogs, and entirely dogless islands such as Aitutaki and Mauke. Mitiaro is an isle of dogs, the oddest ones I've ever seen. It appears as if a German shepherd has been busy fertilising a corgi, producing dogs with huge heads and ears, feet the size of hamburgers, and legs as stubby and bent as bananas.

I'm sure it was these grotesque mutant canines that were responsible for the baying and barking that kept me awake for much of last night. They didn't stop until 4 a.m., when the island's roosters started crowing. They often go together in this part of the world, the dog and rooster duets, a squawking, howling, cacophonous serenade. On islands where there are no dogs, the roosters seldom crow.

Coming towards me now through a shimmer of heat haze is a short, thickset male figure. We draw closer. He is barefoot, smoking, dressed in ragged denim shorts and a filthy yellow singlet. His hair is matted, his facial features bloated, his big bare feet splayed.

'Hello,' he says cheerily.

'Morning,' I reply.

'Staying at Nane's?'

'Yes.'

'You like Mitiaro?'

'I do. It's very peaceful.'

'I'm the mayor.'

'Of this village?'

'Of the island.'

We sit on the grass under a coconut palm and chat. I raise a matter of civic urgency, the unavailability of beer. The mayor grimaces. There *is* beer on the island, he tells me, showing embarrassment, but they're keeping it all for next week, when the prime minister is coming to open the new road. If they sold it now, there would be none for the party when he comes. Normally, he assures me, it would be possible to buy beer.

'Where from?' I ask, as I've not seen a shop anywhere on the island.

'You buy beer,' he grunts, 'at the post office.'

On my last night on Mitiaro I stay in Nane's front room, one end of which is a curtained-off bedroom, the other the island's Air Rarotonga office, which makes my onward flight confirmation simple to effect. After a last walk past the village pigpen, past the huge banyan tree near the waterfront and down to the landing to listen to the waves on the reef, I retire to my bed. There I'm disconcerted for a time by the sounds of Jurgen and Helga's lovemaking coming through the curtain-covered louvre windows at the end of the room. There is a period of peace, then the dogs and roosters start up again.

Mama, Kura, Krissie, baby Kristine and I all leave Mitiaro on the same flight. I'm part of the extended family now, and as I buckle myself into the seat beside Mama at the front of the plane, Kura passes Kristine to me. I hold the baby, who's swaddled in a pink towelling jumpsuit, as we are hurtled down the runway and into the air.

Kristine lies in my arms, her huge brown eyes staring up at me. She seems to be all concentration, and seconds later I understand why. I feel a warm, flowing dampness on my inner thigh – a dampness which makes its way down my leg and into my left shoe. Kristine continues to stare up at me, even as I hold her away and call to Kura for help. Seeing what has happened, Mama cackles gleefully. 'Ah! Mimi!' Kura laughs too, takes the baby and hands me a towel from her bag. 'Sorry about that,' she says. 'We ran out of disposable nappies. And because the post office was closed, we couldn't get any more.'

Mauke is the third of the Three Roots. At the airport I'm met by Tautara Pureau, at whose bungalows I'm staying. He is a tall, jovial man with a small moustache. Although he doesn't tell me this himself, I later learn that he is Mauke's chief administration officer, a man of high standing in his community.

As we drive around a bend at the end of the runway in Tautara's utility truck, I see two well-kept graves, side by side in front of what looks like an abandoned house. To me the letters on the graves seem luminous: ROBERT JULIAN DASHWOOD DIED 1970 AGED 71 YEARS and KOPU DASHWOOD DIED 1984 AGED 66 YEARS.

Dashwood, an Englishman, became a lagoon-side legend in the Cook Islands, living first on Rakahanga in the Northern Group, then on Mauke, marrying on both islands and writing memorably about his life in exile in the South Seas under the nom-de-plume Julian Hillas (his mother's family name). The son of an English vicar, Dashwood was by most accounts a vain, snobbish, eccentric man. The local people named him Rakau, meaning wood. Trader, author and radical politician, Dashwood left an indelible impression on the Cook Islands, but later when I visit the graves and see the empty house I sense a forlorn, melancholy atmosphere about this, his last place of rest. His books, like the man himself, have now melted away into history.

I've picked a good day to arrive on Mauke: the island is playing Mitiaro at rugby, on a field a little way along the road from the Dashwood house. Because of the heat, the game starts late in the afternoon, when the sun drops behind a row of coconut palms which separate the field from the lagoon. The field is mostly grass, with strips of dusty red earth along the sidelines.

A big crowd turns up to watch as the Maukians, in green jerseys, and the Mitiaroans, in black, trot out on to the field. I watch from the top of a bank across the road. The Mauks, who are bigger, faster and better organised, run out to an early lead. They have a small, barefoot, bandy-legged winger, who bolts like a rabbit to score three tries. By half-time it looks as if it will be a rout, and as a recent Mitiaroan I feel a bit disconsolate. Besides, their captain is the island's Air Rarotonga manager, and his office was also half my bedroom. He's a big, muscular guy with coppery hair tied back in a ponytail, and during the breaks he exhorts his team desperately.

This works, to some extent. The Mitiaroans begin to show more determination and some individual brilliance, and they score three tries. But their kicker misses the conversions, two from right in front of the posts, and this brings howls of derision from the crowd. The ponytailed skipper scrags everyone in sight, including the bandy Maukian winger, whom he chases determinedly, overtakes, collars and throws down on to the bare earth. But when the game ends in twilight, victory still goes to the Mauks. The team, and the crowd, are jubilant.

Tautara's bungalows are set out among coconut palms, white sand and tropical gardens a little way back from the lagoon. In the centre is an open-sided, thatched shelter and table and chairs, where meals are served. Staying in the bungalow next to mine is a colossal Rarotongan man with a flat, granite-like face and a lantern jaw. George tells me he used to prop for the Waitemata rugby team in Auckland. Now he's as big as an entire front row and wheezes like a Mac truck's air brakes when he speaks.

Tautara's wife, Kura, lays out a dinner of chicken, fried tuna, sweet potato, tomato salad and fruit. George and I help ourselves, then the big man gives me a nod. 'You say grace,' he commands. I mumble an invocation remembered dimly from childhood, and George nods in approval. Then he picks up his heaped plate and gets to his feet: 'I have to go now, excuse me.' And he waddles off, carrying his dinner before him.

I'm confused. Why doesn't he want to eat with me? Is he taking his meal somewhere else? If so, why? Does he adhere, perhaps, to some bizarre sect which forbids him to share his table with a non-believer? I never found out, but before I left I bumped into George outside our bungalows and asked him if he had enjoyed his time on Mauke. He nodded firmly. 'Oh yes, I like coming here. A nice change, doing nothing.'

'You've been on holiday, then?'

'Oh no, I'm here on business. Working for the government.'

Mauke quickly becomes my favourite of the Three Roots.

It's pretty, completely unspoilt, and everywhere is accessible by bike. There are rain forests and rocky coves and old churches, and it's dogless but not beerless. In the main village of Kimiangatau, opposite the Taunganui landing, there is a sweep of green and two lovely old Catholic churches side by side, one large, the other small, like mother and child.

After borrowing a bike from Tautara, I set off to explore Mauke. There's virtually no traffic, so pootling about on a bike's the perfect way to do it. An east incline takes me about a kilometre inland, where the road forks and there are two other villages, Ngatiarua and Areroa. At the junction of the three roads is a large white Cook Islands Christian church, on the wall of which is painted: 1882 Oliveta Church. The first thing I notice is that there are two long concrete pathways leading up to the side of the church, each of which has an archway above it, and each of which leads to a separate entrance. This must, I realise, be the famous divided church of Mauke.

When the church was planned, the two villages couldn't agree on its interior design. These differences proved irreconcilable, so a wall was built across the centre of the church, and each of the two villages completed its chosen design on its side of the divide. When the acrimony at last was over, the wall was taken down, revealing startlingly different colour schemes and decorations. Today the pulpit straddles the centre, and each village enters by separate doors, sits on its own side and takes turns in singing the hymns. The ultimate example, perhaps, of Christian factionalism.

There are three other European guests at Tautara and Kura's bungalows, backpackers who teamed up after meeting in a hostel on Rarotonga. There's Ian from Stoke-on-Trent, Benny from Copenhagen and Jon from Dallas, all in their early twenties. In the evening we sit around the dining area, drink beer and swap island stories.

Ian's a printer: tall and lean, with cropped brown hair and a slightly bulbous nose. Benny is blond and blue-eyed, very handsome in a Viking-ish way and always smiling. Jon is skinny and rodent-like, with a tangle of long fair hair and slit eyes. They had intended to catch a cargo boat to the Northern Group but it broke down a day out of Rarotonga and had to be towed back to port. So instead they took another supply boat to Mauke, liked the island and have been here for a couple of weeks.

Now Benny and Jon are thinking of moving on, but Ian assures me he's staying put. He loves the island, mainly because he's fallen in love with a girl he met at a dance in Kimiangatau village. Trouble is, he's by no means sure of the local protocol regarding courtship. So when Kura joins us, he says to her, 'What I'd like to know, like, is 'oo should I ask about takin' her to the dance on Friday?'

Kura frowns. Clearly it's a bit tricky, although by no means without precedent. After all, how many other English-men have come to these islands and fallen in love with local girls? Dashwood was the best known, but many of his compatriots have also enlarged the region's gene pool. Kura gives Ian's question full consideration, then replies. 'I think ... first you should ask her father. You see, she works in his shop, and as she is the oldest child, she has most responsi-bility. And because it is her father's business, he is the one most directly concerned. Yes, I think you should first ask her father.'

Ian nods, his brow creased with concentration. He accepts the situation, though obviously he doesn't relish it. 'Okay, okay ... I'll go and see 'im termorrer ...'

My curiosity about this courtship is aroused, so later I bike up to the big old-fashioned shop in the village where the girl in question works. I can see immediately why Ian is smitten. Tara is about eighteen, with long dark hair woven into a plait. She is demure and graceful. Her father is a large man with slightly simian features, who speaks excellent English. We chat while his daughter moves about quietly and purposefully behind the counter, reaching up for tins of corned beef or mackerel from the shelves.

After parking my bike, I walk around to the back porch of a house in Kimiangatau. Sitting on the ground, turning maire leaves into garlands, are half a dozen women and a transvestite. Two of the women I recognise from earlier in the day when, biking through the fernland zone up on the island's plateau, I came upon them plucking the leaves from maire shrubs. There are mounds of maire leaves all around the group. The leaves are smaller but somewhat similar in shape and shade to a laurel. As each garland is finished, it's handed to a man who packs it into a big plastic bag, squashing it down on top of the others.

'What are they for?' I ask one of the women.

'We send them to Hawaii,' she replies, 'for the tourists.'

A tally is kept of each worker's total, then the plastic bags are dispatched to Mauke's airport, and thence to Rarotonga.

In a day they'll be on their way to Honolulu. The Maukians grumble about the mark-up the Americans put on the maire garlands, but it's still a good, reliable export. The consignment I'm looking at, the woman tells me, is worth $3,000–$4,000. And the maire shrub is an obliging partner in the enterprise – the more its leaves are picked, the faster it grows.

Cycling back to the bungalows, I notice on a blackboard by the rugby field the manifest for tomorrow's Air Rarotonga flight out. My name has been chalked on the board, along with several others, including Benny and Jon's, the bags of maire and some taro. In this fashion everyone on Mauke knows who and what is coming and going.

Ian, Benny, Jon, Tautara, Kura and I sit around drinking and chatting in the dining area on the last evening. Benny has only a few days' leave left from his job as a bank teller in Copenhagen. 'When I go back,' he says dolefully, 'I will stare at my computer screen and for months all I will see are the islands of the South Pacific.'

Jon will go on to Aitutaki, but Ian's definitely staying put. There's another dance tomorrow night, and, 'I'm goin' ter try me look one more time.' I don't blame him.

As the maire bags and taro are stowed in the plane's hold, we all climb aboard. George somehow wedges his body into a seat at the front alongside mine. A local man carrying a small plastic bag full of white powder drops it on the floor as he pushes past. It splits open and the powder goes everywhere, but the man appears totally unconcerned. If he is a heroin smuggler, he's very casual about it. One of the pilots sweeps the powder up, and I whisper to George, 'What is it?'

'Starch,' he replies gruffly. 'From the arrowroot. Used for cooking.'

As usual on the outer islands, most of the local population has turned out to see the plane take off. Through the window I can see the tall figure of Ian, standing in the open doorway of the terminal. He gives us one last wave. Then the door is made fast and we taxi out on to the wide, dusty runway. Seconds later Mauke is falling away beneath us: palms, plantations, forest and a pink ring of reef. Then a few wisps of cloud and the apparently endless Pacific Ocean are all we can see.

Back at home I check on the internet for demographic trends on the Three Roots. I find that between 1996 and 2001 the population of the southern islands of the Cook group declined by 26.2 percent. Atiu, which in the 1960s had nearly 1,500 people, in 2001 had only 620. Mitiaro's population has always been small – barely more than 300 – but at the last count had sunk to 250. Only Mauke (700) and Aitutaki (2,322) are holding their own.

As on most of the South Pacific's outlying islands and atolls, the people of the southern Cooks have decided that their future, and that of their children, lies elsewhere, either on the primary island – Rarotonga – or the suburban streets of Auckland. This is understandable, but it leaves me wondering what the Three Roots will be like in another decade, when they're populated only by the very old, and a few young people who dream restlessly of a better life, away beyond the blue horizon.

TWO

MEN BEHIND BARS
RAROTONGA,
COOK ISLANDS

FOR A WRITER to consider the islands of the Pacific is to think mainly of their colonial pasts, of the days when ships, not planes, carried people to them, when writers could abandon their pasts and live in shacks under the palm trees, write by hand in the light of kerosene lamps, send their manuscripts off by sea and, on infrequent visits to the island's only town, rub shoulders and other parts of their bodies with the dusky locals.

The central location for this fantasy is usually a waterfront bar, a dingy establishment with sagging, sandy floorboards where deeply tanned men with bloodshot eyes and murky pasts sit on stools and stare at a row of spirit bottles with stained labels, tormented by memories of those they left behind, or of money-making schemes which came to nothing. The writers' plots are usually melodramatic. The bar is run by an unfrocked priest who lives out the back with a native woman by whom he has had numerous children, and he has an affair with a missionary's wife who cuts the throat of his mistress before slitting her own wrists on the beach. Somerset Maugham and James A. Michener have a lot to answer for.

In real life, most of the bars have gone long ago, or have been spruced up so much that the romance, along with the stained spirit bottles and the tired floorboards, have disappeared. The most famous of all, Quinn's Bar, in Papeete, is no more, although there's a bar by the same name in Papeete's Sheraton Hotel. But here chic couples and French civil servants sip tropical cocktails and nibble on kalamata olives as they contemplate only the menu and the adjoining restaurant's wine list. In the bars of Pago Pago, where Somerset Maugham's histrionic short story 'Rain' is set, the patrons stare mainly at video screens showing gridiron live from places like Baltimore and Cleveland, while even Rarotonga's once-legendary Banana Court today serves mainly lattés and fruit smoothies from its verandah. Only Apia's waterfront road retains a few of the places where classic European human wreckage can be observed amidst a fading décor and tipsy, importuning locals. Recently an extremely drunk visiting European yachtie tumbled to his death from the first-floor balcony of one of the seamier of these bars. All is not yet lost.

Sitting on a plane high above the Pacific, I'm reading an H. E. Bates story set on the island of Moorea. An Englishman lives with an ugly Tahitian woman who loves him but whom he does not love. Eventually she tries to kill him while they're out fishing in a canoe because he has fallen in love with another, beautiful Tahitian girl. After a terrible fight she falls overboard and is mortally bitten by a shark. The story is called 'The Grapes of Paradise', a title perfectly in tune with its melodramatic events, and although the plot is improbable it is entertaining because it conjures up the colonial era so well. It also causes me to regret the passing of the real Quinn's, and other bars, before I had the chance to know them. As I sip Cabernet Merlot at 9,000 metres and listen to Puccini on the plane's headphones, I read, 'He sat in bars on the waterfront and watched dust blow out of potholes in the road outside and then blow back in again.'

Putting the book down, I stare out the plane window. The Pacific looks very close, a deep, clear, inviting blue. All that lies between me and the sea are a few drifts of kapok cloud. My mind dwells on Bates and Jack London and Somerset Maugham and James A. Michener and James Norman Hall and Charles Nordhoff and Robert Dean Frisbie and writers like them who immortalised the old Pacific. Was it easier making a living writing novels when time moved at a schooner's pace and a writer could live well on a dollar a day? In one sense it was: to be a writer then was to be a member of a very exclusive club. A new novel, particularly one set in the South Pacific, was an event, so every novel published stood a decent chance of rewarding its writer. Today the world is awash with novels. Every airport I go to is stacked with the wretched things, flaunting their tawdry covers like harlots desperate for custom. Sometimes I get the impression there are more novel writers than readers.

As I'm lamenting this seismic shift in literary fortunes, the plane makes a perceptible shift in its trajectory. Then, seconds later, through a gap in the clouds, I see my destination, a small green cone, veiled by cloud, encircled by white reef waves. Rarotonga.

First port of call: Trader Jack's Bar and Restaurant. In years to come, this place will probably be as legendary as Quinn's Bar was in the 1950s and '60s. 'Trader's' overlooks the lagoon in downtown Avarua, at the mouth of the Takuvaine stream. The closest building to the sea in Rarotonga's capital, its predecessor was struck by the full force of Cyclone Sally in 1987. A generous measure of the Pacific Ocean poured through the front of the building and passed on out the back, radically rearranging the décor. When things calmed down, owner Jack Cooper decided to rebuild his bar on precisely the same site, working on the theory that lightning doesn't strike the same spot twice.

Lightning, no; cyclones ... maybe. But so far, so good. Big storms have since swept through Trader Jack's, but there are efficient warning systems now so that Jack and his team can shut shop, pack up all the booze, crockery and cutlery, shove them into a shipping container, and move the container inland until the tempest has passed. And the building's strong, no doubt about that. It's tempting fate to call it cyclone-proof, but it's built on piles and is open underneath, so that an angry sea surges through the foundations, rather than the bar and dining area above. And if the storm's not threatening enough to cause an evacuation, there's no finer place on the island than the deck of Trader Jack's to sit and and observe the warning signs: the sky turning the colour of graphite; the glowering clouds moving closer, then dissolving into torrents; the oily waters of the lagoon being cuffed, beaten, then thrashed by the wind. It's like being in the bow of an anchored ship and feeling as well as seeing a storm engulfing the vessel.

But usual weather conditions in Rarotonga are not like that. It is far more typical to sit out on the deck of Trader Jack's in the warm still air of late afternoon, sipping a drink and watching the sun slide down, gilding the lagoon water before turning the sky to a painter's palette, and seeing the glassy reef waves rear, then break on both sides of the place where the Takuvaine stream has made a passage through the coral. Right beside the deck, coffee-skinned local kids cavort in the lagoon, a charter boat unloads its catch, and the paddles of outrigger canoeists dig deep as their slender vessels head out of the tidal basin towards the gap in the reef.

Inside, there's no better place in Rarotonga to rub shoulders with the locals. For Jack's regulars, the bar is the confessional, the marketplace, the stock exchange, the psychiatrist's couch, the gossip column and the Lonely Hearts' service, all in one. It's where all of Rarotonga's movers and shakers hang out, especially on a Friday night. Jack's regulars are today's equivalents of the beachcomber exiles of the old Pacific. They are merchants, hucksters, lawyers, charter-boat operators, retired ships' captains. Men like Don Silk, who for years skippered the inter-island trading vessels which sailed, often under perilous conditions, to the islands of the Northern Cooks. Home from the sea, Don became Rarotonga's harbour-master and wrote a memoir, *From Kauri Trees to Sunlit Seas*, which should become a South Seas' classic, and which he still displays in a case above the bar, autographs and sells. 'You're very lucky, this is the last copy,' Don always tells the person buying the book. Then when they've gone he slips another copy into the case. (There is a persistent rumour that Don is writing a sequel to *Kauri Trees*, entitled *From Sunburnt Knees to Alzheimer's Disease*.)

Then there's Ross Hunter, a giant of a man who looks as if he's just stepped out of a pirate movie. A boilermaker who came to Rarotonga in the early 1970s to help build the airport, Ross stayed on, married a local woman and started, along with an engineering business, what will undoubtedly become an island dynasty. Another fixture at Jack's is Ewan Smith, a pilot who in 1978 began a small airline which grew into Air Rarotonga and today connects over half the fifteen islands of the Cook group. Ewan's also a publisher and a photographer whose camera has captured the character and beauty of even the most remote of the Cook Islands. And no description of Jack's regulars would be complete without mention of Mike Mitchell, lawyer and honorary British consul to the Cook Islands. A bon vivant and raconteur who was best man at my wedding, Mike launched two of my books at Trader Jack's. All these characters were born in New Zealand, but all have sunk their roots deep into the soil of Rarotonga and are in some way inheritors of the great South Pacific dream.

And there are the locals. Men like 'Papa Tom', Sir Tom Davis, scientist, doctor, politician, traditional navigator and author, a patrician figure who, from Jack's bar, will regale an audience on any subject, from early Polynesian dispersal patterns to the right kind of hook to use to catch a mahi mahi.

And George Ellis, descendant of an English trader and his Manihikian wife. A one-time cabinet minister and now a businessman, George is an expert on the black pearls which thrive in Manihiki's lagoon. His children received high qualifications overseas, then returned to help invigorate economic developments in the Cook Islands. And there's Brett Porter, genial, generous and good-looking, who imports most of the meat that's consumed in Rarotonga's hotels and restaurants. It's easy to get the impression that Brett, a man with fingers in many pies, is the de facto prime minister of the Cook Islands.

Sitting at the bar and eavesdropping, I realise that the conversations on either side of me are distinctively Pacific. There is a salvage opportunity after a big yacht was wrecked on Pukapuka. There are rumours about the way prices will go at an upcoming black pearl auction, and the latest developments in the long-abandoned hotel project at Takitumu, and yet more rumours about another shipping venture which is about to be floated, and a new international airline connection to Rarotonga. Everyone has a strong opinion, everyone expresses it, and everyone's opinion is a target for mockery. It doesn't matter that everyone already knows what everyone else's opinion will be, and exactly how everyone else fits into this microcosmic plan. It's all part of living on a tropical island – and one only the size of Wellington harbour.

About 60,000 people – almost all of them tourists – pass through Rarotonga every year. That's a lot of people for an island whose permanent residents number only 9,000. Life on an island whose economy is based on tourism has another odd aspect in that at any given time a substantial slice of the population is in a state of transience. Several times a week a loaded plane slides out of the sky and discharges hundreds of strangers from all parts of the world, who for varying periods of time roam about the island's beaches, reefs, valleys, mountains, villages and bars. A few days later, another plane comes along, deposits another load of tourists and uplifts the previous lot, who within hours are somewhere completely different. This is known as global tourism.

For many of the permanent residents of Rarotonga, monitoring these arrivals and departures involves a degree of social and commercial opportunism. I am in Trader Jack's enjoying an evening beer when Malcolm Laxton-Blinkhorn, ex-minor English public schoolboy, former army officer, former pawpaw exporter and currently an Avaruan motelier, known to his friends as Malcolm Laxative-Bunghole, rushes into the bar. He is clearly in a state of high excitement, his face flushed and his breath coming in snatches as he makes an announcement to the gathered drinkers.

'Slovenian Olympic ski team, came in on the nine o'clock flight. Been training at Queenstown. Here for four days. Eight gels, twelve chaps. *Terrifically attractive*, I hear.'

Even by Rarotonga's thoroughly international standards, this is unusual news. The locals are inured to Americans, blasé about the British, only mildly curious now about Scandinavians, but Slovenia is something else again.

Mike Mitchell turns to me. 'Where the hell is Slovenia?'

'It's in what used to be Yugoslavia. In the north. Next to Italy.' I know this only because I once got to know a very pleasant Slovenian man in a guest-house in Apia. Anton was an agricultural scientist and a painter and he had told me something of his homeland.

'Oh. So where's this team staying, Laxative?' asks Mike.

'At the Edgewater. I'll ring them up and invite them to the Coconut Grove.' He reaches for the bar phone, taps the keys. 'Vaine? Malcolm here. Listen very, very carefully. I want you call the Slovenian ski team and tell them they're invited to the Coconut Grove for a few drinks. By the Cook Islands ice hockey team. When? In ten minutes, Vaine. We'll be there in ten minutes.'

In a remarkably short time we're all crammed into Mike's Nissan and heading off around the island in an anti-clockwise direction, past Avatiu harbour, past the airport, around Black Rock and into Arorangi village.

The Coconut Grove is a cavernous bar, restaurant and small dance floor, set back from the road on the lagoon side. Tonight it has a three-man band, and the music is loud and the lights dim. Sure enough, the Slovenes are there, some of them already dancing. And the rumour about their physical attributes is entirely correct: they are snowtanned, lean, athletic, with short dark hair and shapely Slavic faces. There's just one problem – they're all men.

They're in their early to late twenties, dressed in designer jeans, sneakers, and T-shirts stretched tightly over their bulging pectorals. They are smiling broadly as they dance with the one female on the floor, an Australian woman of about thirty who's already proved herself to be an enthusiastic party girl in her short time on the island. Now she's leaping frenziedly in the centre of the circle of Slovenes, jumping like an aerobics instructor, grinning at each guy in turn, relishing her privileged position. Laxative-Bunghole introduces himself to another team member at the bar and asks, casually, where the Slovenian women are.

'They are very tired. They get off the plane, they go to the beach, then they go to bed,' the skier replies. He looks admiringly at the bouncing Australian. 'But we don't go to bed. Yet.' He laughs in a knowing way, and Jack's team joins in, but very thinly. The news that the female Slovenes have gone to bed is in itself sobering, but the subtext is equally so: these men are so handsome and virile, so athletic, that the likelihood of their women being enticed away from their own kind by a bunch of overweight, middle-aged inebriates is remote.

We have a round of drinks at the bar and glumly watch the dancers. Suddenly, in the middle of a hot number, the Australian woman bursts from her Slavic circle, and jerks her way out the door and into the night. The skiers look momentarily disconcerted, then continue dancing with each other. 'Shirt-lifters, probably,' Mike mutters.

The evening is obviously going nowhere, it's nearly midnight, so I finish my drink and decide to walk back to Mike's place. Outside, along the road a little way, I hear a groaning, and see a huddled figure on the verge. As I approach, the figure gets up from the long grass. It is the Australian woman. She shakes her head vigorously, wipes her mouth and says to me matter-of-factly, 'Ah, that's better.' She gulps, shakes her head again. 'I just chucked.' She takes a few deep breaths. 'Okay now though.' She gasps again. 'Must get back to the Russian spunks.'

And out there on the roadside she starts dancing again, jerking, jumping, snapping her fingers, and in this agitated manner makes her way back into the nightclub.

Next day I'm lying reading on the sand at the end of the little motu, Oneroa, across the lagoon from Muri beach. Between this motu and the next one is a broad, shallow channel of clear water. Looking up, I see two snorkel periscopes approaching, two prone, flippered figures moving lazily through the waters of the channel until they're just a few metres from where I'm lying. One figure, then the other, rises from the water. Both remove their flippers, masks and snorkels and wade ashore. I recognise the man as one of the Slovenes who was in the Coconut Grove last night. The woman with him is clearly another of the Olympic ski team.

She stands at the water's edge, mask in hand, looking about her, and I'm immediately put in mind of that unforgettable scene from the first James Bond film, *Dr No*, in which Ursula Andress emerges from the tropical sea, in Jamaica or somewhere. This woman, who must be about twenty-five, has the same proud stance, the same tall, perfect, athletic body. Her hair is blonde too, and hangs in wet strands over her finely deported shoulders. But there's one startling difference. This statuesque woman is naked from the navel upwards, and her high, firm, dripping breasts are two of the most spectacular natural features I've ever set eyes on in these islands.

Wading back across the lagoon, I pass several more snorkelling Slovenian women, none so handsome or strikingly unclad as Ursula, but all strongly built and obviously relishing their South Seas stopover. And back on Muri beach I pass the whole Slovenian men's team playing volleyball. Most of them are wearing only shorts, and their bodies are unbelievably muscular — shoulders as wide as doors, thighs like barrels, stomachs flat as planks. All that slaloming and poling across mountainsides must be a powerful bodybuilder. Certainly these skiers are magnificent physical specimens, and I have to stop and watch them for a while.

Just to top things off, they're good volleyballers too, fast, limber, with fine hand-eye coordination. As they serve or volley or spike they shout, laugh and call across the net. Their language, which sounds rather like Russian, is spoken with feeling and accompanied by much waving of their powerful arms.

Eventually it's time to get back to Trader Jack's, to watch another sunset and catch up on the latest bulletin of news. The Slovenians are already history. They'll be on a plane out soon, and gone forever. But tomorrow or the day after others will be dropping out of the sky to take their place, to excite the expectations of the locals. A netball team from Barbados, perhaps, or a film crew from Rome, or a bevy of models from Berlin. We raise our glasses to the prospect.

THREE

A REAL HEROINE
AITUTAKI,
COOK ISLANDS

AITUTAKI IS TO RAROTONGA what Capri is to Italy: a beautiful, accessible tourist playground just a short trip from the mainland. Forty minutes by plane from Rarotonga, its main attraction is its huge lagoon and a string of ten islets – motus – along the lagoon's eastern fringe. The main island, which lies to the west of the lagoon, is pendant shaped and rises to a height of just 124 metres. The population of Aitutaki lives in several villages on this island, where the airport is also located, but the motus are uninhabited, just like the desert islands of romantic fiction.

However, one motu, Akaiami, for a time had an international airport terminal. During the 1950s Aitutaki's lagoon provided a landing strip for the Tasman Empire Air Lines' Solent flying boats, which plied the so-called Coral Route from Auckland to Tahiti via the lagoons of Fiji, Samoa and Aitutaki. These cumbersome but comfortable planes flew across the South Pacific at low altitudes – their cabins were unpressurised – and the little island of Akaiami had a jetty where the planes tied up for refuelling. During the brief stopover the passengers – the Solents carried up to forty-five people – could stroll about the creamy sands of the motu or wander through its lushly vegetated interior for a few hours. Travel on the Coral Route was expensive at a time when most international passengers went by sea, and many of the world's rich and famous stepped from a Solent and on to the sands of Akaiami.

The Coral Route was a romantic way to travel, but by the late 1950s sealed runways had been built at Nadi, Papeete and Rarotonga, and Aitutaki's desert-island airport had become obsolete. Today, though, Aitutaki is flourishing again as planes fly to and from Rarotonga several times a day, bringing tourists from all over the world to stay in resort hotels, motels or backpacker hostels. But in spite of its popularity and many visitor arrivals, Aitutaki remains unspoilt and laid-back. For West Europeans in particular, it conforms perfectly to their vision of a tropical South Seas island.

Best-known of Aitutaki's motus is One Foot Island, or Tapuaetai, which lies at the south-eastern corner of the lagoon. It looks like a human footprint when viewed from the air, and is surrounded by golden sands. Legend has it that a man was forced to flee across the lagoon to the little island with his son, his mortal enemies in pursuit. After first walking behind the boy to conceal his footprints with his own, and so deceive the enemy into thinking that there was only one person on the island, the father hid the boy in the top of a palm tree. The footprint ruse worked: the father was caught and killed, but the boy went undiscovered and survived.

Some years ago I wrote a short story which evolved into a novel for young adults. It was about a teenage girl from Aitutaki who, being top of her class in all subjects at her island high school, was sent to Auckland by her family so that she could fulfil her academic potential. Life in the big city for the girl, whom I called Tuaine, was disastrous. Living with relatives who had little money, she was cold, homesick and lonely, and had to steal a jacket from a department store to keep warm in the Auckland winter. Apprehended after feelings of guilt drove her to return the jacket to the store, Tuaine just avoided being brought before the court. The novel ended with the girl opting to return to her island to live and complete her schooling. I called it *Leaving One Foot Island*. After it became a set text in some secondary schools, I considered writing a sequel. But what could possibly happen next to Tuaine, back on her idyllic island home? I needed a narrative implant, but one wouldn't come.

Then I was commissioned to write the text of a large-format book called *The Cook Islands*. Lavishly illustrated with photographs by aviator Ewan Smith, who has lived on Rarotonga for many years, the book covered the island nation's history, geography, customs, fauna, flora and art. Many of Ewan's photographs, particularly those of the Cook Islands' remote Northern Group, were strikingly beautiful. After the book was launched with due ceremony and celebrations in Rarotonga, Ewan and I flew to Aitutaki to carry out a small marketing exercise. We sold a respectable number of books there, as the island was given generous coverage in both text and photographs. Among those who bought a copy was a local girl of about twelve, who asked shyly if we would sign it for her father and mother.

Dining that night at a local resort hotel with some of the locals, I found myself sitting next to a pleasant, middle-aged Aitutakian woman. We chatted about the island and, in particular, the prospects for its young people. The woman commented, 'There's a problem for our young people in that they often meet other young people visiting from overseas countries, and they become restless and want to leave.' She smiled sadly. 'Just recently the sixteen-year-old daughter of a friend of mine fell in love with a boy from a visiting yacht. He wanted to stay on Aitutaki and be with her, but his parents disapproved and he was sent back to California, to go to university. My friend's daughter was heartbroken.'

I caught my breath. At a stroke, serendipitously, I had an idea for the sequel to *Leaving One Foot Island*. And as soon as I got home, I began to write it.

In the sequel, Tuaine meets an Australian boy, Adam, while she is sailing on the lagoon and he shows off to her on his jet-ski. After they get to know each other better, Tuaine takes Adam sailing to Akaiami and One Foot Island, and they share the pleasures of her island home. Tuaine is fearful that Adam will discover the secret of why she had to leave Auckland, but this concern is overshadowed by the dis-approval she receives from Adam's parents. His family are Jewish, and for their only son to have a relationship with a Polynesian girl is not in their plans for his future. Adam runs away with Tuaine to One Foot Island and she hides him there, but his sanctuary is only temporary and the novel ends with his family insisting that he return to Melbourne and begin a law degree. He does so, leaving Tuaine distraught.

I called the second book *Return to One Foot Island*. But clearly, it too demanded a sequel. Again I gave considerable time and thought as to what could happen next. As often happens with fiction writing, my invented character, Tuaine had become such a presence in my imagination that she practically stalked it, demanding that her dilemma over Adam be resolved.

Then, not long after I had sketched out some ideas for the third novel, I again visited Aitutaki, to write a travel story about a couple of new resorts which had opened there. One of the resorts, Are Tamanu, was a little way out of the main village. I parked my rental car beside a small reception building by the entrance and was somewhat surprised to see a teenage girl lying sound asleep on a couch under the eaves of the building. Slender and barefooted, with long black hair, she was wrapped in a pareu. As there was no one else inside the building, I coughed a few times and she woke, sat up, stretched and smiled apologetically. And there before me was Tuaine, the living embodiment of my imaginary heroine, a girl so like my fictional character it was scary. I could hardly believe my eyes.

Tripping off ahead of me, down a concrete path between coconut palms and bungalows, the girl led me to the resort bar, at the top of a bank overlooking the lagoon. There she poured me a beer and explained that her parents who ran the resort were out, so she was in charge for the afternoon. She was in the sixth form at the local college, she said, and her name was Eikura Henry. 'Related to the first prime minister of the Cook Islands?' I asked. I was aware that Albert Henry had come from Aitutaki. 'Yes, he was my great-grandfather,' she replied languidly. Very pretty and utterly natural, she was still blinking away the vestiges of sleep. And as she did so I was thinking, *No, your name's not really Eikura Henry, it's Tuaine Takamoa. You are exactly as I've always imagined Tuaine to be.*

'Why have you come to Aitutaki?' Eikura asked me. When I told her I was writing a story about the island, her eyes widened. 'You're a writer? What's your name?' I told her and she gave a slow nod of recognition. 'I met you once before,' she said coyly, 'when you and Ewan Smith came to Aitutaki with the big book about the Cook Islands. I bought a copy and you signed it for my mother and father. I was about twelve, I think.' Then she added, 'And we study your *One Foot Island* novels at school. Are you going to write another one? We all wondered what Tuaine did after Adam was sent back to Australia.'

I didn't tell her how much like Tuaine she appeared to me to be, but I did say that if they ever made a movie of the books, they need look no further to cast its heroine. When copies of the third book in the trilogy, *The Pearl of One Foot Island*, arrived from the publisher, one of the first people to whom I sent an inscribed copy was Eikura Henry of Aitutaki.

FOUR

THE MISS TUTTI FRUTTI CONTEST
SAMOA

THEY ARE SEEN throughout the islands of the South Pacific, the people known variously as fakaleiti (Tonga), raerae (Tahiti), tutu vaine (the Cook Islands), pinapinaine (Tuvalu) and fa'afafine (Samoa). A third sex, they attract much curiosity from visitors, a fact they don't seem to mind at all. Since the time of first contact, these people have drawn the attention of European travellers. James Morrison, the twenty-seven-year-old boatswain's mate on William Bligh's ship *Bounty*, who joined the mutiny and wrote a journal documenting the ill-fated voyage and the extraordinary events surrounding it, included this description: 'In Tahiti they have a set of men called Mahu. These men are in some respects like the eunuchs in India but are not castrated. They never cohabit with women, but live as they do. They pick their beards out and dress as women, dance and sing with them and are effeminate in their voice. They are generally excellent hands at making and painting cloth, making mats, and every other women's employment.'

Other recorders of early contact with traditional Polynesia, including Bligh himself, commented on the third-sex
phenomenon. According to these accounts, Tahitian mahu
were limited in number and were chosen by their families to
take a female role from an early age. Bligh was sufficiently
interested to closely examine some mahu. He reported that
their genitals had been pulled back between their legs and
also appeared to have shrunk. Other men, Bligh recorded,
derived sexual pleasure from the mahu, and there was no
stigma attached to being one. In fact, some mahu used their
status for self-advancement. Many were esteemed servants
to chiefs, who were prohibited from having female servants.
Glynn Christian remarks of the mahu in his book *Fragile
Paradise*, 'Most were available for sexual purposes, but only
performed fellatio.' From the mahu evolved their contemporary equivalent throughout French Polynesia, the raerae,
or transvestites.

Naturally extroverted and demonstrative, the transvestites
of Polynesia are an intriguing social and cultural phenomenon.
Although sometimes the butt of coarse jokes in their com-
munities, they are tolerated in a way that they are not in
western society. Often large and powerfully built, they are in
manner and temperament thoroughly female. Even after years
of observing these men-women, it still disconcerts me when
a young man with the physique of an All Black flanker approaches my restaurant table with a mincing gait and a flower
behind his left ear and asks, in a lilting descant, 'Sir, would-
you-like-something-to-trink?' I know one versatile raerae,
employed as a cultural attendant on a cruise boat in the Society

Islands, who each evening entertains his passengers by demonstrating skills ranging from basket weaving, pareo tying, ukulele playing, tamare dancing and, on the last night aboard, the modelling of a range of elaborate wedding gowns. Over two metres tall, the flamboyant Tomita obviously adores her work.

In Samoa the fa'afafine (the expression means 'to act like a woman') are ubiquitous. Surprisingly, in a society in which sexual mores still border on the Victorian, they attract little derision or condemnation, perhaps because they have been part of Samoan society far longer than the Christian scriptures. Commonly, and somewhat annoyingly for heterosexual men, the prettiest women are drawn to their company. And every September in Apia, Samoa's capital, the nation's leading fa'afafine compete for the coveted title of Miss Tutti Frutti, one of the two climaxes of the annual Teuila Festival. (The other is the Miss Samoa contest, a much more conventional and very protracted beauty pageant.)

The teuila is Samoa's national flower, a member of the ginger family. With its long scarlet bloom made up of delicately layered petals, it resembles a burning brand. Both the flower and its elongated leaves are much favoured by those who decorate Samoa's churches and hotel lobbies. The festival named after it is hugely enjoyable – a sort of Rio carnival, Henley regatta, Hero parade, Mormon Tabernacle Choir and one-day cricket tournament rolled into one – and many expatriate Samoans, of whom there are now tens of thousands, return to their homeland for its full week of cultural and sporting activities, which include kilikiti (Samoan cricket), fautasi (canoe racing), church choirs, street parades, brass-band contest, outdoor variety concerts, craft and art displays – and the two beauty contests.

This year Miss Tutti Frutti is being held at the Hotel Kitano Tusitala. The hotel has a vague Robert Louis Stevenson theme, but the great Scottish teller of tales would be spinning in his tomb up on Mt Vaea if he could see what was happening. More than 2,000 people have turned up; hundreds more have been turned away. Most have to stand, as there are not nearly enough seats. The catwalk extends well into the audience, which clamours with anticipation as the start of the contest approaches. The lyrics of a suitably plaintive song boom out from stereo speakers, 'I AM YOUR LAY … DEE … AND YOU ARE MY MAA … AA … NNNN', before Tanya Toomalatai, the Mistress of Ceremonies, announces the first act. Tanya, a melon-breasted, gravel-voiced Amazon in a pastel-blue micro-skirt, is the size of a lock forward in Manu Samoa, the national rugby team. Describing herself as 'the whore from Hawaii' – where she lived for some years – she invites the audience to 'laugh with us, not at us', and draws sincere applause. Then the first dancers glide on to the stage.

They are a troupe from Pago Pago – American Samoa – and they are breathtakingly beautiful, with brown hourglass bodies, lustrous waist-length hair, huge dark eyes, dazzling smiles and gorgeous yellow costumes. Garlanded in frangipani, their dance is more Tahitian than traditional Samoan, their sinuous movements perfectly choreographed as they raise their bare arms and reach for the stars. In astonishment I say to the Samoan man standing alongside me, 'I can't believe these creatures are really men.' He laughs delightedly. 'Settle down mate, these are girls. This is just the curtain-raiser.' A strange kind of relief passes over me.

When the real contestants swan on to the stage, the difference is very apparent. The MC announces each of the thirteen, then one by one they strut their stuff. They have names like Cindy and Dolores and Cleopatra. Some have breasts, others are more gamine; some are tall and well built, others slender, or avocado-shaped. All are outrageously flamboyant, dressed like peacocks in brilliantly coloured, inventive costumes. As they come down the catwalk they wiggle their hips, pirouette, then present their rumps to the crowd, which roars its appreciation. The raunchier the presentation, the louder the applause. Tanya becomes very worked up. 'Here is Blondie. Her statistics are 22–44–88. Give her a big hand. But not the way we do.'

After the tutti comes the frutti. The contestants do their second presentation festooned with grapes, apples, oranges, pawpaws, pineapples and, in one case, bananas – strung across the contestant's loins like a tropical sporran. Wearable *and* edible art. The audience greets each contestant with hoots of approval.

While the judges, seated at the end of the catwalk, go into a huddle to decide the winner (there are very strict criteria, one judge tells me later), Tanya gives a condom-fitting demonstration on a donkey-sized dildo. At the sight of this the audience is in an uproar, howling with laughter, almost helpless with shock and delight. It is then that I realise that the Miss Tutti Frutti contest is a kind of safety valve for the spectators, releasing some of the pent-up tensions in a society in which piety and its associated double standards too often rule.

There is a serious subtext to the evening, too. One of the beneficiaries of the pageant's gate-take is an HIV-AIDs awareness programme. Already there are officially twelve cases of HIV in Samoa, possibly more. Tonight's contest – which carries an R16 restriction – raises $22,000 tala (dollars) for the cause.

Whether in rugby, choral singing or cross-dressing, Samoans are the most fiercely competitive of all Pacific peoples. The result of the Miss Tutti Frutti contest is eagerly awaited, and when it is announced that the winner is the generously proportioned, banana-wearing 'Blondie' (aka Alosina Ropati), there is widespread approval.

Later I interview Ken Moala, one of the organisers and himself a fa'afafine, who tells me that in pre-European times the fa'afafine were the entertainers of society. 'They were considered very creative, artistic people and were accorded great respect. The Miss Tutti Frutti contest is a portrayal of our lifestyle, not a beauty pageant.' As for the vexed question of how the fa'afafine come about, Ken's response is unequivocal. 'We are born that way,' he declares. But when I mention this to a fa'afafine I know well, he rolls his eyes in exasperation and pronounces archly, '*Well*, you can't believe everything *he* says.'

Preparing for take-off from Faleolo Airport a few days later, the flight attendant going through the safety routine is a big-boned, handsome young Samoan man with shiny black, cropped hair. He looks somehow familiar. Was he in one of the canoe-race teams I watched getting into their boats at the bottom of the steps opposite Aggie Grey's? Or maybe he was one of the airline crew by the pool at Aggie's yesterday. The young man takes off his lifejacket, buckles himself into a cabin crew seat and sits bolt upright as the noise from the plane's engines intensifies. Seconds later, the plane is hurtling down the runway.

This is a daylight flight, so when the plane banks over the Apolima Strait between Samoa's two main islands, there below us is the 'big island', Savai'i, its great volcanic backbone and forested slopes clearly visible. The island's highest peak, Mt Silisili, rises to over 1,800 metres, while on the north-eastern slopes the dark patches of its lava field stand out starkly.

When another of Savai'i's volcanoes, Mt Matavanu, erupted between 1905 and 1911, lava from its crater flowed down to the northern coast, causing the population of villages in its path to be evacuated before the flow eventually solidified. It left behind a landscape that looked like a vast slab of black toffee, whorled and twisted into fantastic patterns. Walking across this lava field is like being on the planet Mercury, the temperatures are so hot, the landscape so harsh and barren. It was near there that I once stayed in a most interesting hotel, the Safua. Interesting not only because it was situated so close to Savai'i's huge lava field and natural swimming pools, but also because I met there for the first time that most bizarre of human animals, a husband-and-wife pair of social anthropologists.

I had first heard about this species from a Tongan man, who told me that anthropologists were forever coming to Tonga to research some aspect of traditional life. One had come from a university in Chicago to live in his village on Tongatapu because she was writing her doctoral thesis on Tongan funerals. She stayed in one of the village houses, waiting for someone to die. Months passed, and nobody did. The Tongan man shook his head in disbelief. 'She watched everyone every day for signs of ill-health, especially the old people. But everyone stayed healthy, and the healthier they were the more pissed-off she got.' He laughed, sardonically. 'I thought she would poison one of us, just to get the funeral she wanted. But when we went on living, she packed up and went off to Eu'a, because she heard that someone in a village there was dying.'

I thought this sounded like a tall story until I met the couple at the Safua. They had come to Savai'i because they knew it was a place where fa'a Samoa – the traditional Samoan way of life – was still strong and relatively unchanged. But were they researching traditional Samoan customs or art? No, they were writing a book on suicide in the South Pacific.

Gerhardt and Ula were German, from Berlin, and they had the fanatical, humourless, narrowly focused attitude of academic researchers everywhere. He had a long fair moustacheless beard. She had a round pale face and blinked constantly. It occurred to me as we spoke over dinner that a century earlier they would probably have been missionaries, seeking souls rather than suicides. Only when the subject turned to self-killing did Gerhardt become animated and voluble.

'In Fee-gee zay are mostly using veed-killer, vee haff found, especially za Indians. In Papua New Guinea, though, zay are nearly alvays us-ing guns. To za head, in most cases. Here though, in Samoa, vee are finding zay are mostly hanging theirselfs.'

'Yah,' put in Ula, 'so for our thesis, vee must ask ourselfs, vat is der reason for zees differences? Vat is za pattern in all zees suicides?'

When I asked these professional voyeurs and documenters of human misery how long they had been working on the research, wondering what the long-term effects of such a study would be on their psyche, Ula replied, 'Oh, a long time, now. Vee haff grants from many universities, to carry out our verk. Alvays, vee are traffelling in za islands. Vee haff been on za run for … for … eight years now. Next, after Samoa, vee go to Wanu-atu.'

'Veedkiller there too, mainly, zay say,' Gerhardt put in thoughtfully.

After Savai'i has receded into the distance and we have levelled out high above the clouds, the handsome flight attendant refills my wine glass. He is very attentive and considerate. 'You like this wine, Sir?' he inquires softly. 'I do, yes, thank you.' As he bends and carefully pours the merlot, I am struck by a gust of aftershave lotion. It has the tangy smell of ripe tropical fruit. Glancing upwards, I notice too that the young man has a touch of mascara under both his eyes. And in that moment I realise where I have seen him before. At the Miss Tutti Frutti contest. Wearing pawpaws.

FIVE

MOST TREASURED ISLAND
SAMOA

'I SHOULD LIKE TO RISE and go / Where the golden apples grow, / Where below another sky / Parrot islands anchored lie.' Robert Louis Stevenson wrote these lines as a young man, the son and grandson of lighthouse engineers, growing up in Scotland. His dream of leaving his wintry homeland and fetching up on 'parrot islands' was realised when he and his wife Fanny and her two children arrived in Samoa in 1889. He was thirty-nine years old. He was to spend the last six years of his life there, and the couple's tomb lies high up on forest-covered Mt Vaea, overlooking Samoa's capital, Apia. Stevenson was already a world-famous author when he came there to live. A tuberculosis sufferer, he needed Samoa's balmy climate to ease his suffering and prolong what he well knew would be an attenuated life. The Samoans came to revere him, calling him Tusitala – 'Teller of Tales'.

The name Vailima, which Stevenson chose for his mountain home, is seen everywhere in Samoa today as it's also the brand name of the nation's beer, which is brewed on the outskirts of Apia, in a building complex even larger than the largest of the country's many large churches. Vailima means 'Five Rivers', a reference to the network of natural water-ways which cascade down the slopes of Mt Vaea. So every time I have a beer in Samoa (and it's a very hot country, so a high fluid intake is necessary), I think of Robert Louis Stevenson. And every time I visit Samoa, I have to climb Mt Vaea and visit the writer's home.

Four years before he arrived in Samoa, Stevenson had written to a friend, the poet W. E. Henley: 'Do you know anyone that wants a cough: a hacking, hewing, tickling, leacherous, choking, nauseating, vomitable cough; a cough that springs like a rattle, rakes like a harrow and deracinates the body like a stick of dynamite?' His solace, however, was that 'when I spit blood I write verses'. Several times during the 1880s he nearly died, his tuberculosis compounded by sciatica, and an eye infection which almost blinded him, but amid the blood-spitting and verses came his most famous prose fiction: *Treasure Island* (1883), *The Strange Case of Dr Jekyll and Mr Hyde* (1886) and *Kidnapped* (1886).

A few years earlier, in France, he had met and fallen deeply in love with Fanny Osbourne, an American divorcee of Dutch extraction, ten years older than him and the mother of two children, Lloyd and Isobel. After tenaciously following Fanny to America, Stevenson wooed and married her, in 1880.

In the late 1880s the couple and their large entourage sailed in a chartered schooner through the Pacific in search of their ideal island refuge, calling at Hawaii, the Marquesas, the

Tuamotus and Tahiti. Stevenson found all these islands lovely, but he settled on Samoa because, it has been claimed, the postal service there was more reliable. As a serialising novelist who depended on episodic publication to provide his income, Stevenson needed the service of the mail-boat that called regularly via Auckland or Sydney.

The Stevensons arrived in Apia nine months after a terrible cyclone had destroyed several German and United States warships anchored in the town's harbour. One hundred and forty-six men had perished. Only the British battleship *Calliope* was saved. While the Germans and Americans didn't want to lose face by weighing anchor, the British captain did what every capable skipper knows must be done when a cyclone strikes: he got back out to the open sea. The carcasses of the doomed vessels, *Olger*, *Adier*, *Vandalia*, *Trenton* and *Nipsic,* still littered the reef and beach when Stevenson and his family sailed into Apia harbour.

The family took accommodation in a two-storeyed harbourside hotel. It's still there. Today the upstairs area is occupied by Sails, a high-quality restaurant and bar; while downstairs is a rough bar, Bad Billy's, one of the last in the South Seas' tradition of such dives.

The balcony of Sails restaurant is a great place to have breakfast. I sit and look out over the sea wall, the row of big pulu trees that have withstood a dozen cyclones, and Apia harbour, where a few overseas yachts are bobbing at anchor, their prows turning into the trade wind. That the building is truly historic can be judged from its colonial architecture and wildly undulating wooden floors. A young, handsome Samoan lays a huge plate before me: eggs, hash browns, sausages, tomatoes, bacon and pawpaw. 'Enjoy your prekfast, sir,' he says shyly. There's enough here to feed a family, and it takes me a good while to make any impression on it at all. But I'm in no hurry, and while I eat and look out over the town harbour, I'm thinking of Robert and Fanny, who must have enjoyed this view too, and of the political crisis which had then engulfed this part of the South Pacific.

When they arrived the whole Samoan archipelago was in political turmoil. The world's three great powers, the United States, Germany and Britain, were desperate to gain ascendancy, then annex the islands for their own purposes. They have been described by one historian as being, 'like three large dogs snarling over a very large bone'. The analogy is only half apt. The dogs were indeed large and certainly snarling, but the Samoa islands could more suitably have been likened to chunks of prime fillet steak. There were thirteen of them altogether, and three – Tutuila, Upolu and Savai'i – were large. All were fertile and ripe for plantation purposes. Copra and palm oil, present in large quantities, were in great demand in Europe. Apia on Upolu, and especially Pago Pago on Tutuila, had fine harbours, and the latter was the perfect site for a coaling station to refuel naval battleships in mid-ocean.

Robert Louis Stevenson was quickly apprised of this tense situation by a man who was to become his soul mate. H. J. Moors was a roguish American who had jumped ship in 1875 with a bag of onions and a chest of cloth. With these minimal commodities he had set up a trading store on Savai'i before moving to Apia, where he married a local beauty and became a gunrunner for one of the pretenders to the non-existent throne of all Samoa. Moors had read all of Stevenson's books and was something of a writer himself, so he was on the beach when the Scots novelist and poet stepped ashore.

Moors made the arrangements for Stevenson's purchase of 300 acres on the eastern flanks of Mt Vaea, a few hundred feet above the sea, where it was cooler. The whole area was covered in tropical rain forest filled with lupe – wild pigeons – and other birds, including the lovely scarlet-headed cardinal honey-eater, called by the Samoans segasegamauu. At Mt Vaea the writer had indeed found the 'parrot islands' of his youthful fantasies. And it was here that he and Fanny had built, from cedar imported from Canada, the grandest house in the South Pacific islands. In one downstairs room they even had a brick fireplace, to remind them of northern winters, but in Samoa's sweltering climate it was said never to have been lit. The kitchen was a small detached building, kept a distance away from the main house to minimise the risk of fire.

The Samoans, many of whom could now read and write through the zealous efforts of the missionaries, were fully aware of Stevenson's stature and proud of the fact that he had chosen to live among them. Resilient, and adaptable in the way of most transplanted Scots, Stevenson not only had an engaging and generous disposition towards the local people but also read the Samoan political situation cannily.

In the early 1890s the Samoans as well as the Europeans became engaged in a bitter power struggle. Although there had never been a single ruler of all the islands, the United States, Germany and Britain were determined that there should be one – and one of *their* preference, so that they could pull the puppet's strings and get their own way. The two contenders for Samoan kingship were Mata'afa and Laupepa. Moors supplied Mata'afa with firearms to fight Laupepa, who was elderly and dispirited. Stevenson, too, recognised that the locally popular Mata'afa was more up to the job and rallied behind him. This was appreciated by the Samoans, but not by the European pooh-bahs in Apia, who were doing all they could to aid Laupepa.

In 1893, on the eve of a battle between Mata'afa and Laupepa, Stevenson and his stepson Lloyd Osbourne rode down from Vailima to view the preparations, which Stevenson would later describe in vivid detail in his work *Footnote To History*. It is an unsentimental account: for example, although he greatly respected the Samoans, he abhorred their custom of degrading their foes by decapitating the vanquished and presenting the heads to their leader.

Despite the troubles, back up on the hill at Vailima life continued contentedly enough. Stevenson's health had improved markedly. He was still frail but did not let this prevent him from horse-riding, dancing, beachcombing, kava drinking or smoking. The family enjoyed musical soirées in the dining hall, where there was a roller organ; Stevenson himself played the flageolet, a small flute. They also entertained lavishly. Stevenson had a large Samoan household staff whom he dressed in kilts of Royal Stuart tartan. (After all, a kilt is just a tartan lavalava.)

There was another very Samoan aspect to the Stevenson household which the locals were not slow to appreciate. Robert and Fanny had brought their extended family to live with them – Fanny's two children and, later, Stevenson's Scots cousin Graham Balfour and pious old Presbyterian mother. It was a clan gathering, a Scots aiga, (Samoan for the extended family), and the civil war being waged in Samoa may well have put Stevenson in mind of the highland clans he romantically admired.

In the evenings the household sang, dined, partied and welcomed everyone except the sour consuls from Germany, America and Britain. Stevenson had it made known publicly that he disapproved of the actions of these men, being both shrewd and imaginative enough to understand that they were acting entirely out of self-interest. In the meantime, Samoan war parties, faces blackened, would ride up and drop into Vailima for kava, food and political discussion. Stevenson led an unashamedly seigneurial existence, but everyone liked him. He was hospitable, generous and courageous. He wrote in the mornings, sitting up in bed, fearing that another haemorrhage would strike before he completed his magnum opus, the novel *Weir of Hermiston*. Later in the day, he would walk in the nearby forest, listen to bird songs and no doubt contemplate his life, work and mortality.

The Samoans were not so sure about Fanny. She had a dark complexion and an enigmatic half-smile. They called her Aolele, or Flying Cloud, because of her changeable expression, but she was a formidable presence who ran the large household efficiently and nursed her husband with great tenderness.

Mata'afa lost the war of 1893 and was banished to Micronesia. The chiefs who were his supporters were jailed. Stevenson took them food, kava and tobacco. When they were released, they greatly improved the muddy track leading to Vailima, in appreciation of his patronage. It was named the Road of Loving Hearts. When it was opened, Stevenson made a moving speech (oratory was another of his skills) in which he entreated the Samoans to use their country wisely, and to care for its lands and forests, otherwise 'others will'. It was a prophetic warning.

Less than a year later, on 3 December 1894, Stevenson died suddenly from an aneurism. He was forty-four, and *Weir of Hermiston* was unfinished. The same chiefs who had built the Road of Loving Hearts cut a path up Mt Vaea, and young warriors carried his body to a clearing, where he was buried. The ashes of Fanny were later buried beside him, following her death in California in 1914.

Six years after Stevenson's death the trio of great powers got their way when, in an arrangement of breathtaking brazenness, Germany annexed the western islands, the United States took control of the eastern group, and Britain cried off in exchange for taking over the external affairs of Tonga. Vailima became the official residence of Dr Solf, the governor of German Samoa. The Western Samoans were not to rule themselves again for sixty-two years.

In 1991 and 1992 two vicious cyclones, Ofa and Val, assaulted Samoa. Vailima, by then the official residence of the Samoan head of state, was badly knocked about. Enter, in 1993, a group of Mormon businessmen from Utah. They bought the house from the government for a token sum and planned its refurbishment as a literary museum. They also planned to build a cable-car to whisk tourists from Apia up the slopes of Mt Vaea to Stevenson's tomb. Vailima was to be turned into a Robert Louis Stevenson theme park.

Protests at such tackiness were aired, and the cable-car scheme was dropped, but radical renovations to Vailima went ahead and were completed by December 1994, the centenary of Stevenson's death and the occasion of much memory-raising. Professional Scotspersons from all over the world made the climb up Mt Vaea and heard Stevenson's poem and epitaph, *Requiem*, read in highland cadences by the Scottish actors John Shedden and John Cairney.

Today there is definitely no need for a cable-car; every second car in Apia is a beaten-up taxi. Breakfast over, I hail one and it takes me up the Cross Island Road to Vailima. Just weeks ago another cyclone – this one called Heta – whipped the north coast of Samoa, and I am anxious to see what effects it might have had on the foliage and the house. But the driveway is pure beauty: long, straight, and with luxuriant tropical shrubs, flowers and trees crowding in upon it. At the end the road curves, and there, set amid a vast expanse of lawn, is Vailima: cream painted, two-storeyed, red roofed, balconied, its verandah bracketed. It is a hot morning, and too early for Mt Vaea to cast shadow across the treeless lawn, on which brown birds called vea peck happily. The Samoan flag hangs limply above the roof in the mid-morning sun. Above the front door is a large sign: VILLA VAILIMA. Why villa? I wonder. For the

Mormons to ensure that it wasn't mistaken for a lager advertisement?

As I approach, a young and very pregnant Samoan woman greets me, speaking with an American accent. Explaining to her that I will climb the mountain first, then see over the house, I ask if Cyclone Heta has damaged the tracks. 'Oh no,' she replies, 'they're fine. I suggest you take the short track up, and the long track down. Then it's about forty-five minutes up and about thirty-five minutes down.'

Crossing one of the crystal-clear streams that flow down the mountain, I begin the climb. It might be short, but it's zigzagging, very steep, studded with volcanic stones and strewn with leaf litter. In minutes I am saturated in sweat, and have to stop every five minutes or so to catch my burning breath. I am surrounded by forest giants – great buttress-rooted trees whose canopies block out the sky – while sleek, iridescent black skinks like komodo dragons freeze at my footfall, then dash up the nearest tree-trunk. In the smothering heat, the going is extremely tough, and for a time I think I won't make it. But I must. After one last gruelling zig, followed by one final exhausting zag, I emerge on to a cleared promontory, and the tomb is before me.

It's well worth it. No one else has made the pilgrimage today, so I have the sanctuary to myself. A cooling breeze sweeps over the clearing, from where there are views of Upolu's northern coast, the horizon gauzy with mist, the lagoon and reef, Apia town and, by swivelling to the south, Vailima and its expansive grounds. Stevenson must have been able to look up from his bedroom and see this place where he would be taken and buried. The only sounds up here are the soft calls made by the unseen lupe, the pigeon which makes its home in the forest. Now I can see, across the face of the distant mountains, the destruction that Heta has caused. Striations in the forest show where the trees have been swept aside and turned to matchsticks by the winds howling inland, then being forced up with intensifying fury. Turning my back on the view, I walk over to the whitewashed concrete tomb. Regrettably, its sides have been defaced with graffiti, which no one has made any effort to cover. Trying to ignore the graffiti, I concentrate instead on the bronze inscriptions. First, the immortal *Requiem*:

> *Under the wide and starry sky,*
> *Dig the grave and let me lie.*
> *Glad did I live and gladly die,*
> > *And I laid me down with a will.*
>
> *This be the verse you grave for me:*
> *Here he lies where he longed to be;*
> *Home is the sailor, home from the sea,*
> > *And the hunter home from the hill.*

The definite article in the second to last line shouldn't be there: Stevenson wrote 'home from sea'. But it would have been a costly business fixing a typo cast in bronze, so if you insist on the correct version you have to see the one by the gate, at the entrance to the Road of Loving Hearts.

On one end of the tomb, too, is Stevenson's somewhat uxorious tribute to Fanny:

Teacher, tender comrade, wife,
A fellow-farer true through life
Heart-whole and soul-free,
The August Father gave to me.

The slow track down Mt Vaea follows the back side of the mountain, and has long reaches doubling back on each other. As I make my way down, I realise that the pregnant woman at Vailima hasn't climbed the mountain for a while, for obvious reasons, because the track down *has* been damaged. In fact for some reason Cyclone Heta has done more damage to this side of the mountain. Many great trees have been torn out by the roots, leaving huge sockets in the earth. Where their trunks have fallen across the track, someone has sliced them up into rounds with a chainsaw, but the rest of them lie prostrate, already being overtaken by regenerating under-growth. The track is muddy, and in one place has been washed away completely, leaving a huge diarrhoea-like streak through the forest. I have to make my way across it by swing-ing from tree root to tree root like a nervous Tarzan. It's a relief when I at last reach the bottom, cross the stream and walk back up to the house, unsteady with fatigue and smeared with ginger mud.

A young Samoan man shows me through Villa Vailima, starting with the living room. Its walls are lined with tapa cloth, and there is an enormous lioness skin on the floor. In one corner is the virgin fireplace. Upstairs are the bedrooms and Stevenson's library, which also contains a bed. Beside this bed is a special stand on castors, which enabled him to write while he was confined to his bed. Here too, in glass cases, are the many editions of his works, translated into several languages, and first editions of the four books he wrote while living at Vailima. Tastefully restored, the rooms contain period furniture, sketches done by Isobel and others, and many photographs.

Downstairs, linked to the upper level by a grand twisting staircase, is the great dining hall. A huge room, it has wainscoted walls, bare polished floorboards and, at one end, a long dining table. There is a bronze of Stevenson on another table, and his portrait in oils hangs from the wall beside his big iron safe, which the Samoans used to eye apprehensively because they believed that therein lived Stevenson's fictional demon, the Bottle Imp. Hanging from the walls are more photographs: of Stevenson lighthouses; of the author with prominent local matai (Samoan chiefs); with his good mate, Moors; with another friend, King Kalakaua of Hawaii; with Fanny, Lloyd, Isobel and Stevenson's mother, Maggie. In all the photos it is Stevenson my eyes are drawn to. His frame is wasted but he is elegantly dressed and his gaze is fresh, youthful, penetrating. And between his fingers, always, there is a cigarette burning, just as his lungs must have been.

Stevenson wrote a second stanza to *Requiem*, which for years was missing. It reads:

> *Here may the winds about me blow;*
> *Here the clouds may come and go;*
> *Here shall be rest for evermo,*
>> *And the heart for aye shall be still.*

At the end of the strenuous day, I pour myself a glass of cold Vailima, look up from my hotel balcony and watch the rays of the sinking sun lighting up the forest trees across the face of Mt Vaea. I raise my glass in the direction of the mountain. Thank you, Robert Louis Stevenson, for Jim Hawkins, Blind Pew and Long John Silver, David Balfour, Dr Jekyll and Mr Hyde, the Bottle Imp, and all your other characters who will live in our minds forever.

Ia manuia, Tusitala!

SIX

SUNDAY, BLOODY SUNDAY
TONGA

I T'S ELEVEN O'CLOCK at night and I'm waiting for a taxi outside Fua'amotu Airport in Tonga. I'm here to write a book about this, the only kingdom in the South Pacific, starting on the main island, Tongatapu. A sagging Toyota taxi emerges out the warm, still darkness and I hail it. I don't know anyone here, and one of the few pieces of information I have is the name of a Nuku'alofa guest-house, given to me by the Canadian engineer I sat next to on the plane.

All I can see of Tongatapu is that it's flat, has many palm trees, and the roads are long, straight and potholed. The driver and I make desultory conversation, then his car radio begins to crackle. Voices come on, then are replaced by others. Many of the callers – it's obviously some kind of talk-back programme – seem very excited. One word is repeated by every caller. *Pa'anga*.

'What's happening?' I ask the driver.

'The mini-games. These people, they call the radio, they say how much money they give for the mini-games.'

Mini-games? A contest for small people? Or possibly small games – table tennis, marbles, arm wrestling, petanque – for ordinary-sized people.

'What are the mini-games?'

'Games for people from all over the Pacific. Guam, Vanuatu, Cook Islands, Pup-oo New Guinea. Every four years they have South Pacific Games. Every two years we have mini-games.'

'For all Pacific countries?'

'Pretty much. But not for Australia and New Zealand.' He chortles. 'They too big for mini-games. Too much people.'

'What sort of games will you be having?'

'Tennis, golf, athol-letics, volleyball, netball. Lots of games, hundreds of people.' Voices are still coming through the radio static. 'That's why people are ringing up. To give money. Mini-games costs a lot of money.'

The guest-house, located in a leafy street deep in Nuku'alofa, supplies me with a room with a concrete floor, many louvre windows, a large bed and a private bathroom. The room opens on to the courtyard of a large rambling house with numerous semi-detached units set among banana palms and hibiscus bushes. Weary from an excess of inflight food and drink, I go straight to bed. To bed, but not to sleep. All night dogs bark and bay, while in the unit next to mine a group of happy evangelical Christians from the United States sings songs praising the Lord until three in the morning. When at last the dogs and Christians have run out of steam, the roosters take over. One crows continuously for two hours, just outside my window. I get about thirty minutes' sleep in all. At seven o'clock I get up, check out and call a taxi to take me to the Keleti Beach Resort.

The Canadian also mentioned Keleti Beach. 'It's outa town but it's quiet, and the beach is kinda nice. American-run, too.' Quietness is a priority right now. Writers immerse themselves in quietness, breathing it in and converting it into books. The photosynthesis of silence. The only book I could have written in that guest-house would have been entitled *How to Murder a Cock/Dog/Christian*.

I'm still in splenetic mood as I'm driven out of Nuku'alofa and along other straight, flat roads lined with long grass and palm trees. Then we come to what is clearly an arterial road, and turn on to it. As we pass a large stadium, the driver, who so far has not spoken, says, 'That is National Stadium. New. French gives us money for it. Mini-games start there tomorrow.'

It certainly looks impressive, the high grandstand, the big all-weather track, the line of flagpoles. If there is time, I might go and have a look at the athletics, I think idly. Then the taxi turns off this main road and along an unsealed one, then off the unsealed one and along a dirt track which runs between unfenced verges of rank grass. At the end I see a plywood sign, hand-painted in blue. *Keleti Beach Resort*.

Just inside the entrance to a one-level, breeze-block, louvre-windowed building is a reception desk and a small lounge containing a round plastic table and chairs. A series of shells on vertical strings makes a kind of curtain between reception and a large, concrete-floored courtyard. The wings of the buildings lining the courtyard have wide eaves sheltering rows of metal tables and chairs, and rows of coloured light-bulbs are strung across the yard. Through the far end of the courtyard I can see the horizon, a line of streaky cloud and the brilliant blue sea.

Behind the L-shaped reception desk is a woman of about fifty-five. She has brown hair tied back in a bun, skin the colour of putty and spectacles with very thick lenses. A fold of white skin under her chin, and a wide, tight mouth, give her a frog-like appearance. Her upper arms are broad, with bags of flesh hanging from them, and she has a paperback novel in one hand and a cigarette in the other. Looking up, she gives me a tight smile. She has light blue eyes. Very calculating light blue eyes.

'Morning.' Her accent is American.

'Hello. Do you have a vacancy?'

'We sure do.'

She sets the cigarette down on a clamshell ashtray. 'We can do you a whole fally fer thirty puh-ungas a night, haff a fally fer twenny-five puh-ungas, or a dorm-it-tory room for ten.' Dormitory has a boarding-school ring to it, but this is neutralised by the ten pa'anga aspect. I'm a budget traveller, so I ask to see the dormitory room. The woman leans back and calls imperiously at the shell curtain: 'Ladu!'

A Tongan boy of about sixteen, curly-haired, handsome, well built, with a smooth, shapely face, appears. He is wearing a yellow T-shirt, blue lavalava and jandals. The woman passes him over a key.

I follow the boy down a descending concrete path lined with red and yellow crotons. At the bottom is a custard-coloured, two-storeyed building with a flat sloping roof and a concrete terrace along the front. Behind the building is a cluster of towering coconut palms, and in front of it a sweep of lawn from which sprout small palms and hibiscus shrubs. Latu unlocks the end door of the building and I walk in.

The room is narrow but contains two beds – one on either side of the room – made up with blue linen. The floor is bare concrete and there are louvre windows at the front and rear. Under the window by the door is a small table and a chair; behind the door is an open rail from which hang a few wire coat hangers. The room is cool, it has everything I need, and I can hear no dogs, roosters or evangelists. Through the front window there is an agreeable view over the garden and the sea beyond. And all for ten pa'anga.

'Bathroom is along there,' explains Latu, smiling.

'It'll be fine, thanks. I'll come up and sign the register when I've unpacked.'

I walk out on to the concrete terrace. The sky has turned grey but it's very warm. Below me the grass slopes away to an area planted thickly in banana palms and aloes. To my right a concrete path undulates up to several well-spaced oval fales with yellow walls and roofs of red-painted corrugated iron, like the helmets of conquistadors. The reception block and dining area up to my left are ramshackle, but the profusion of plants and palms softens their unsightliness. And, although I can see a harem of scratching, pecking chickens guarded by a ginger-plumed rooster down on the grass, there is no noise except the regular rising and falling of the nearby sea.

I set off down the lawn to investigate. A sandy track passes between boulders of black basalt. Tiny mercurial skinks dart left and right to get out of my way. The track opens out on to a small beach at the foot of a basalt escarpment about five metres high. The surface of the sand is still damp from dew, but underneath is soft and warm. Sinking down into it, I stare out at the sea.

The lagoon is narrow and carpeted with coral, twisted into myriad shapes. Clear, sandy-floored pools separate the ridges of coral, ascending in a series of steps to the reef itself. On the top the reef is level, but on the landward side it is terraced, resembling a line of little ziggurats. In front of these terraces is a pool of calm, clear water, and skeletons of dead coral, jagged and brown, protrude from the white sand.

My eyes are drawn to the terraced reef. The sea is surging and foaming over and through it, exploding upwards in a series of continuously performing blow-holes. It is like watch-ing a long line of fountains programmed to play at slightly varying intervals. The water looks irresistible, but my bathing togs are not yet unpacked. Later, after I've set up my room, I'll swim. But still I make no move, and it is another half hour before I tear myself away from the hypnotic sight of endlessly surging, erupting sea.

It's Saturday today. Tomorrow, the South Pacific sabbath, the shops will be closed, so if I want to see Nuku'alofa properly I'd better do it today. There is a resort mini-bus that goes to the town but I've missed it, the woman at the desk tells me. Her name is Joyce, and when she sees that I've put 'writer' on my registration card she's suddenly very friendly. 'Did yuh bring yuh books with yuh? There's just no damn books in this country. I read everything – always have – but here? Just fucking Bibles.'

I offer to lend her some novels, and ask how I can get into town. She suggests a taxi. Then I notice an old bike in the yard. Could I borrow that? Sure, sure …

With a decent bike, Tongatapu Island would be ideal terrain for a cyclist. There are few hills and not much motorised traffic. But this bike is way past its best. It has no brakes and has long been a stranger to an oil can. I don't think it's been ridden more than a few hundred metres since Queen Salote was on the throne. Still, it gets me along a lot faster than walking.

The greyness has gone from the sky, replaced by a deep blue and traces of high, feathery cloud. I follow Joyce's instructions, and cycle along narrow, dusty white tracks between long grass and scruffy palm trees until I join the main road. There I'm overtaken by big crammed buses, whose passengers peer at me through the open windows. Beside the road, children stop and stare as if I've got two heads. Cycling cannot be a common form of transport in Tonga, I conclude.

Nuku'alofa is a dusty, old-fashioned town with narrow streets and crooked, two-storeyed buildings. Everything looks old and run-down: the wooden buildings, the vehicles, the merchandise in the shadowy shops. There are lots of people standing about, looking as if they have nothing much to do and all the time in the world in which to do it. Most of the men are smoking. But there is something so sleepy and unhurried about the town that it is instantly appealing. It would be the perfect location for a movie set in nineteenth-century Mexico. I prop the bike up against a fence, buy a

Coke from a streetside food stall and sit at a rough wooden table to drink it.

Watching the people standing about or strolling past is an absorbing pastime, and as I'm doing so I realise there is an influx of visitors. Young men and women dressed in brightly coloured tracksuits are wandering about among the locals. They must be the mini-games athletes. Their tracksuits proclaim their nationalities and sports. There are netballers from the Cook Islands and athletes from Vanuatu; weightlifters from Nauru and tennis players from Tahiti; boxers from Papua New Guinea and golfers from Guam. They walk along the street with an easy, lithe gait, looking as if they just can't wait to run, jump, hit a ball, press a weight or pin an opponent to a mat.

Watching these young athletes gives me a new appreciation of Pacific solidarity. They are here not just because they are athletes but because they are people who inhabit a special region and feel part of it. Some are Melanesian, some Polynesian, some Caucasian; others are of mixed race. What unifies them is the ocean which surrounds their island homes.

The bike has now become an encumbrance. I can't leave it anywhere because it doesn't have a lock and chain, and, lacking brakes, it can't be ridden in traffic. So I walk and push it down Taufa'ahau Road, across the intersection of Wellington Road to the waterfront and along to the Royal Palace.

The traditional rulers of Tonga – the Tu'i Tonga – went back 1,000 years; the present monarchy goes back only to Tonga's 1875 constitution. This was written by an ambitious Methodist missionary called Shirley Baker (a man), and enshrines absolute power in the monarch, his appointees and thirty-three 'noble' families. All land is owned by the monarch, and about 100,000 commoners vote for just nine of the thirty parliamentarians. So grateful was King George Tupou I of Tonga to his missionary friend for securing the throne for the house of Tupou that he made Shirley Baker minister of foreign affairs, comptroller of the revenue, and premier of the kingdom. This did not endear Shirley to all Tongans, and in 1887 he only just survived an assassination attempt.

Now, at the beginning of the twenty-first century, Tonga retains its feudal system, and is ruled by the ailing Taufa'ahau Tupou IV, who succeeded his much-loved mother, Queen Salote, in 1965 and is now 86 years old. The monarchy, modelled firmly on the English system, is these days heavily criticised by educated expatriate Tongans, who decry the lack of democracy and absence of press freedom enshrined in the constitution. Although the king remains popular with commoners, the momentum for social and political change is slowly building, and will undoubtedly come to a head after his death.

The palace building, set on a velvet lawn, is not large as palaces go, but it is stylishly colonial, with white walls, red roof, fretwork around the verandahs, finials and ornate bargeboards. Palace guards in immaculate white jackets, red-striped trousers and smart hats eye me with more than a passing interest as I lean the bike on a concrete gatepost and peer at His Majesty's pad. One guard has a bright fixed bayonet on his rifle. These chaps look as if they're very keen to enforce the kingdom's status quo, so I decide to push off.

Back at Keleti Beach I set up my laptop on the table under the front window of the dormitory and plug it into a power point. I've purloined a table of the right height from the dining room. The bottom of the window is level with my chest, so that I can see out over the lawn, palms and basalt boulders. There is a peep of the sea and a sweep of sky, the first ultramarine, the second powder blue. It's serene and beautiful, and soon I'm typing conscientiously, glancing up periodically for refreshment, like a swimmer taking breath.

After I've filled my self-imposed 1,500-word quota, I get up from the table and stretch. The palms are casting long shadows across the grass as the sun sinks in the sky. It's been a gruelling day, what with biking and writing, and I decide to lie down on the bed for a late-afternoon nap. In a few minutes I've dozed off.

'Aaah … aaah … aaah … aaah …'

Appalling sounds, unmistakably of human suffering, shatter my sleep. They are coming from the other side of the concrete-block wall to my right. As I sit upright, the choking is replaced by a dire groaning.

'Uuuh … uuuh … uuuh … *Jesus Christ* …'

Good God, what is happening in there? Is someone being murdered, or is it suicide? I get up and put my ear to the wall. There's a crash, followed by a snapping of wood – is furniture being broken? – then a groan. Then, a period of silence, followed by horrible snoring. The snoring gets louder, and my concern is replaced by resentment. That's just what I need: a vomiting, snoring drunk for a neighbour. As I get ready to go and have my evening meal, I resolve to move further down the dormitory to get away from the swine who's disturbing my peace. After locking my door, I pause and peer in through the louvres of Room Two. All I can see in the darkness is a broken bed on which is huddled a shadowy figure whom I guess to be male.

The Keleti Beach dining room is long and rectangular, lined with louvre windows and tapa-patterned curtains, and with real cloth stuck to the walls. Latu, now dressed in a white long-sleeved shirt, tupenu (a dark skirt) and jandals, is a very attentive waiter. As well he might be, for apart from me there are only two other diners, a couple.

The man is in his early fifties, big, with slicked-back hair and a large, slumped stomach. He smokes continuously, even as he eats. He looks to me like a Darryl. The woman is plump, with long brown hair, and wears a short-sleeved blue cotton frock. She can be no older than twenty. She looks down all the time, and barely utters a word when he speaks to her. She looks like an Angela. There is a melancholy air about the couple. Are they father and daughter? I don't think so. Although there is a certain similarity about them, the way Darryl looks at her is not the way a father looks at his daughter. Lovers, then? Probably. The presence of the odd couple stirs my curiosity. Where did they meet? By the water dispenser? In the factory canteen? At the photocopier? What did he say to get her to come away to Tonga with him, a man three times her age?

After the meal I walk across the courtyard and into the lounge. It too is a long narrow room with louvre windows. It contains a few well-worn vinyl sofas and chairs, a TV set and DVD player, and french doors which open out to a broad verandah. On the verandah I can see a table-tennis table and some weightlifting equipment. At one end of the lounge is the bar. It has a small horseshoe-shaped counter, above which is a sheet of steel reinforcing mesh, painted cream, in which a head-sized hole has been cut. Behind the mesh is a man of about sixty, and in front of it, sitting on a stool, a much younger man. With the steel grid between them, they look as if they're in a Central American prison on visiting day.

As I approach the bar, the older man looks up and says in a drawl, 'How yer doin'?' Joyce's husband, I presume.

He is scrawny, slack-shouldered, balding, with folds of skin hanging from his turkey neck. A cigarette droops from a corner of his mouth. I order a Royal beer, posters for which I have noticed in the town, and he ambles off down a passage and opens a fridge. The man on the stool looks at me crookedly. He is about thirty, with cropped brown hair, a fleshy, flushed face, and brown eyes. He wears a tight white T-shirt and cheap-looking jeans. His eyes seem to be having trouble focusing. Blinking hard, he shakes his head as if trying to dislodge water from his ear, then peers at me.

'Ow's ut going', thun?'

'Not so bad, thanks.'

'Jost arrived, 'ave yuh?'

'Last night. From Auckland.'

'Me too, jost arrived. I'm frum Brimming'im. Ing-lund.'

'That's a long way from Tonga.'

'Bit of a boos ride, yus. Me name's Rob.'

As we shake hands, the barman returns with beer and pours it into a plastic cup. I try it. It's dry and well chilled, and has a pleasantly hoppy after-taste. I see from the label that it's brewed in Tonga, 'with Swedish assistance'. I say to the Englishman, 'That's good beer, don't you think?'

'It's all right, yus. I've 'ad worse, like.'

'Do you live here, Rob?'

'Me? Shit no, oim jost vistin'. Oi luv in Feegee.'

'What's that like?'

'VB Bitter. All VB Bitter.' He belches and pushes his plastic glass under the grill. 'Same again, thanks Bill.'

Not quite understanding, I ask him, 'Have you seen much of the Pacific?'

'Seen it awl, mate. Bin everywhere.'

'I'm going to Samoa for my next trip. What's that like?'

'Vailima. Not a bud brew, neither. Gerries do thut wan.' He puts one hand flat down on the bar for a moment, to steady himself. His face has gone a terracotta shade. Frowning now, he continues, 'Least ut's Vailima in Apia. In Pago ut's Bud-weiser. American there, y'see.' He rolls his eyes ceilingward, recites: 'Niue, Steinlager; Tahiti, Hinano; Raro-tong-ga, Heineken.' He belches again, interrupting the litany of lager. 'Bot doan't go ter fookin' New Cally-doanya. Yer cun't get a decent beer there. All woine. Too many Froggies, y'see.' Looking perplexed now, he peers through the mesh at Bill, who's pouring him another Royal. 'Bot Tahiti's Froggie too, und they've got beer there. Hinano. Foony, thut is. Why is thut, Bill? Why cun't yer get a decent beer in New Cally-doanya?'

'That is something,' the barman drawls back wearily, 'that I just can't tell you. Only place I ever bin to in the Pacific is right here in Taang-ga.' With extreme lethargy and much sighing, Bill tells me his background. He and Joyce had run what he calls a 'sanitorial maintenance operation' (could he mean cleaning business, I wonder) in Chicago, but the Illinois winters had got too cold for them. So they read books on the Pacific, decided on Tonga, wrote to the government, and were offered a two-year work and residence permit if they would run the Keleti Beach Resort. They sold up everything and came here six months ago.

'So how do you like it?'

Bill sucks his gums, swallows, pulls at the crepey skin on his neck. 'Wal, it is warmer than Chicago, no question 'bout that. I mean, the john hasn't frozen over here yet ... But as far as the tourist trade's concerned ...' For the third time he leaves his sentence unfinished, and instead looks out over the lounge, leaving its emptiness to speak for itself. I feel sorry for him, and as an expression of sympathy order another two beers for Rob and myself. As Bill brings them, I say, 'Are you staying in one of the fales, Rob?'

'Fook no, oim in the dorm-it-tory block down the path.'

'Oh? What number?'

'Noomber Two.'

I pause, look at him intently. 'Did you arrive late this afternoon?'

He grins inanely. 'Thut's right.' He blinks with the effort of recalling even his recent past. 'Uctually, I was a bit pissed. 'Ad a few too many beers on the plane, like. Thun I 'ad a ruff taxi ride 'ere, and chooked oop in me room.' He brings the lager up to his lips and sips gratefully. 'Oim all right now, though. Now oiv 'ad a few beers ...'

I like the Keleti Beach Resort. It doesn't bother me that it has Albanian architecture, or that it's way out of town. It's quiet working in my dormitory room (Rob hasn't vomited or collapsed the furniture again), the food is tolerable, the beer cold, and when the words don't flow I just get up and stroll down to the little cove and watch the sea making fountains through the blow-holes. What is strange about the place is that it has so few guests. They can now be counted on the toes of one and a half feet, because Darryl and Angela have folded their tent and stolen away in the night.

They've been replaced by a trio of beautiful young Italians – two men and a woman, all in their early twenties – who look as though they might be filming a Louis Vuitton advertisement. The Italians breakfast early, radiating a style and sophistication that looks out of place in the concrete and plastic dining room, then vanish in a taxi, returning, still radiant and voluble, as the sun is going down. Apart from this stunning *ménage à trois*, there is Rob, me and a sweet, darkly tanned Danish couple who are so ancient and wrinkled they look as if they've been dug out of a peat bog in Jutland. They totter to the beach in the morning, sleep in the afternoon and watch old films in a corner of the lounge each evening.

Rob is a drunk, a no-hoper and a layabout of the first order. I like him a lot. I like his dark sense of humour, his fecklessness, anarchy and total dedication to the booze. There's something likeable about a thorough, amusing drunk, the way he lives for the day and so obviously relishes getting totally pissed at every opportunity. At any time from breakfast onwards, Rob is at the bar, swaying on the stool in front of the steel reinforcing mesh, waving his glass about as if he's conducting the Birmingham Symphony Orchestra. And as he drinks he expounds on his life in the Pacific.

'Oi loov Feegee, y'gnaw? Oi live in a village, a little village, wiv the chief – the rut-too's daughter. She … what the fook's 'er name again? Hahahahahaha … She's all roight, y'naw? I still cun't think of 'er name, but it'll coom it'll coom … Anyway Graeme, oim a sparky by trade, a nelectrician, so oim a bit oova magic mun like, t'the Feeg-geeans, to the fuzzee-wuzzees. Oi fix their videos und their toasters and thut, und when oi do, they give me presents, like a case of VB Bitter. Hahahahaha …'

It isn't hard to picture Rob in 'his' village, lurching about among the empty VB cans, mending the occasional fuse or broken iron to demonstrate his magic: reprehensible behaviour in one way, but in another just part of an old English colonial tradition involving the white man who is a failure at home but an outrageous success in the outermost reaches of the Empire. He will eventually drown in a lake of lager, and it will be the most pleasurable experience of a short, untidy life which has overflowed with self-indulgence and self-abuse.

But I get the impression that for Joyce and Bill life has been long and largely luckless, and that one of their unluckier decisions was the one to leave the United States and move to Tonga. For Joyce this realisation manifests itself in a rejection of all things 'Taan-gun' (even after a year in the country, she can't pronounce its name properly). At every opportunity she rails against the people, the climate, the politics, the economy, the king, the church, even the food: 'Do you know that last year the Taan-guns had to import coconuts from the Cook Islands? *Coconuts!*'

Bill, in contrast, is afflicted with a tiredness which is exhausting to watch. Everything he does is done slowly and to the accompaniment of signs and groans. Even when he sits at reception, glumly reading a novel I've lent him, he groans every time he turns the page, not over the progress of the plot (it is a Maurice Gee novel), but with the extreme effort it requires to move on to the next page. I don't think Tonga has done this to him. Bill looks the sort of guy who was born exhausted.

Then, on my fourth morning at the resort, as I walk past reception on my way to breakfast, I am startled to see that Joyce is transformed. She is vivacious, goggle-eyed with joy.

'Guess what, Graeme? Guess what?'

'You've found a Tongan you like?' I feel like replying, but instead I say lamely, 'I've no idea, Joyce.'

She makes little clapping movements with her hands. 'The whole fucking Pap-oo Noo Gin-yin mini-games team is comin' here tonight fer a party! A hunert and twenny of the mother-fuckers!'

She pours out the details. The Papua New Guinea team has booked in for dinner at seven o'clock. After the meal there will be a dance. But why the Keleti Beach Resort? I can't resist asking. Unoffended, Joyce explains that no other place on the island would take such a large group at short notice.

'Wow,' I reply, impressed but still doubtful. 'Can you cope with as many as that?'

Joyce's eyes retract, her lids half close. 'At forty puh-ung-ga a head, we'll fucking well cope, all right.' She leans across the desk and calls out to where Bill is readying the van for a trip into Nuku'alofa for supplies. 'Bill! *Bill*! Soy sauce! Don't ferget the soy sauce! Twenny bottles!'

Later, as I sit at the bar after a long day at my laptop, Rob raises his glass. 'Bula vinaka, my son.'

'And malo ei lelei to you, Rob. Had a good day?'

'Aw yeah, not so bud. Few beers after breakfast, bit oova kip after loonch, game o' table tennis wiv Latu, few more beers after thut. Now oim all ready for the party. 'Av you seen what's 'appening outside?'

Rob leads me to the windows of the lounge. At the far end of the concrete quadrangle, above the cliff that faces the sea, a number of men are busying themselves with microphones, amplifiers, drums and a big switchboard. Flex entrails cover the floor, and big speakers have been set up on either side of the thatched shelter.

'Who are they?'

'Pup-oo New Gin-yins. Boogers uv brought their own bund.'

Three coaches pull up, and the partygoers – groups of young men and women dressed in vivid red and yellow track-suit tops, black pants with red patterned stripes up the sides, and dark-coloured sneakers – enter the resort tentatively, self-consciously. Their faces are coal-black, their hair frizzy, their teeth almost luminously white. Many of the men are shorter than the women, but they're perfectly proportioned, muscular and neat, while the female team members are lithe and slender. Latu, in bright white T-shirt bearing a Keleti Beach logo, tracksuit pants and white sneakers, ushers the guests to the metal tables around the quadrangle. He is assisted by a small European boy, a Palagi, in a tupenu and Roman sandals. Both of them carry woven pandanus trays.

Soon the tables are full, men on one side of the quadrangle, women on the other. It's dark now, and the coloured lights are switched on. There are no festivities yet; the team members just sit, sipping Coca-Cola or cream soda from the can, occasionally standing up to photograph one another. Each flash of the camera is followed by a burst of mirth and the exposure of teeth as dazzling as the flash.

Rob and I take a seat at a table near the reception area. Rob is growing very agitated. He nudges me excitedly as the women continue to crowd into the courtyard. 'Hey, look ut thut wun over there, look at the boom on 'er! I never seen so mooch bluk velvet together in wun place ...'

A tall Melanesian man in a green blazer steps up to the microphone, and the team quietens in a moment. Speaking first in pidgin, then in English, he calls for 'impeccable behaviour, self-discipline, good sportsmanship and total commitment'. Then he steps back. 'I now have much pleasure in calling upon our minister for sport, culture and youthful affairs, the Right Honourable George Banuba!'

Sustained applause greets the movement to the microphone of a tall, heavily built man in white dinner jacket, grey needlecord trousers and open-necked, floral-patterned shirt. He wears tinted glasses and has a bushy black moustache. On behalf of his government he welcomes the team to the games and also calls sternly for impeccable behaviour, self-discipline, good sportsmanship and total commitment.

'Any team member not behaving in accordance with these rules –' he pauses, and his audience exchange nervous glances or stare at the floor – 'will, I assure you, be ... *finished.*' Allowing another long pause, he glowers at the crowd, then his big fleshy face breaks into a broad grin. 'But for now, we can eat, drink our soft drinks, and dance. A good games to you all!'

Joyce and her kitchenhands have worked some sort of miracle. The dining-room tables sag under platters of taro, breadfruit, marinated fish, chop suey, cold chicken, cold pork, fresh vegetables, rice, baked beans and a variety of salads. Latu moves proudly among the guests, helping with plates, glasses and chairs as the team members line up for their buffet meal. Joyce, standing by the kitchen door, scrutinises the table through her thick-lensed spectacles. She wears a long black halter-necked dress, and is smoking feverishly. Bill is nowhere to be seen.

Joyce beckons me over, and speaks from the side of her mouth. 'They're quite little, you notice that? They probably won't eat that much. And their manners, I really like their manners. Not like Taan-guns. You ever seen Taan-guns eat?' She spreads her bare arms wide and makes huge sweeping gestures towards her mouth, from which her cigarette dangles. 'Taan-guns eat like this.' She makes the sweeping movement again, removes the cigarette, works her mandibles as far as they will go, then shuts them. 'That's how Taan-guns eat.'

After queuing up too, I take my plate out to where Rob is sitting and casting giddy looks over the women in the crowd. The food is mostly heavy, but tasty enough. Certainly the Papua New Guineans are showing total commitment to the meal. And in one respect Joyce is right: they are an extraordinarily polite and well-behaved group. They laugh and chat, but there is no rowdiness of any kind. Usually when I've heard mention of Papua New Guinea it's been in association with the 'rascals', and their brutal raping and bashing activities around Port Moresby. But these people constitute the most respectful and self-disciplined sports team I've ever seen. They're also very happy; it shows in their beaming faces and their open laughter. The PNG mini-games team are having the time of their lives.

At the far end of the courtyard the band launches into a reggae number, and several of the Papua New Guineans leap up and begin to boogie. In some cases the men cross the yard and choose a partner; in others women get up and dance in a line without male assistance. The dancing snowballs and in minutes the joint is jumping.

The Right Honourable George Banuba is sitting at a table beside mine and Rob's. With him are three strapping, unsmiling young men in pale brown safari suits. The minister seems in semi-jocular mood, tapping one foot to the beat, but from time to time he frowns and sweeps the dance floor with his gaze, searching for any breach of good conduct. Rob returns from the bar with four bottles of Royal lager and lines them up carefully on our table. Slopping some into his glass, he asks me: 'Well, 'av you enjoyed the Keleti Beach Resort thun, me old Kiwi mate?'

'I have, Rob, I have. I mean, it's not the Sheraton, but it's been good enough for me.'

Then he holds an imaginary microphone in front of my face. 'And what do you think of Tong-ga, Sir?'

I clear my throat. 'There's nothing wrong with Tonga that a decent revolution wouldn't fix.'

'Hahahahahaha ... thank you sir, end of interview. You uv bin shot, decup-i-tated und yer 'ead stook on the front of 'is Majesty's suff-fari wuggun.'

Crimson-faced, Rob rocks back on his chair, attempting at the same time to focus on the people on the now-crowded dance floor. He tips his seat back too far, rocks forward, regains his balance and his glass, but in the process slops beer over his hand and on to the designer trousers of the Right Honourable Minister at the next table.

As Rob's chair legs crash back to the floor, the minister rises very slowly, very deliberately, making broad sweeping strokes with one hand to remove the lager from his thigh. He then stands over the Englishman, glowers down on him from what seems an enormous height and says in a tone of un-mistakable menace, 'I think ... that you ... have had ... too much to drink.'

Rob swivels in his chair and looks up. He stares at the burly politician for a few moments, getting him into full focus, then says in a tone of total nonchalance, 'Und I think ... that you ... ought to go and get fooked.'

As one, the three minders rise from their seats and advance. At the same time the minister's right hand reaches for the back of Rob's shirt. Jumping up, I slip between the Papua New Guineans and Rob, who has calmly turned back to attend to the balance of his drink. I hold both my hands up to the minister, who looms as large and menacing as a grizzly bear.

'It's okay, it's okay, he didn't mean it, really ...'

The hostility in the minister's eyes diminishes, and his hand drops to his side. As it does so, the other three men halt their advance.

I go on. 'I'm sorry about your trousers, but let's not let it spoil a great party, okay ...'

The minister stands glaring at Rob for a little longer. His big chest rises and falls steadily. Suddenly his face breaks into a gap-toothed grin, although his brown eyes remain un-amused. 'And they always say,' he says, 'that it is we *natives* who can't hold our liquor.'

The band gets louder, the dancing more joyful. The whole courtyard is a seething mass of grinning, jigging, twisting tracksuited figures. Cameras flash as the team members put the party on record. Rob grins, digs me in the ribs.

'Not a bud mob, are they? Hey, look ut her ...' He points admiringly to a petite, shapely girl of about eighteen, dancing at the end of a line of swaying female athletes. She is dark, lissom, surpassingly pretty. Rob's eyes bulge. 'Cor, oi wouldn't mind playin' hide-the-sausage with 'er.' He waves at the girl, who turns away in embarrassment. Rob subsides into deep thought.

'Do you know, oi've never fooked a white woman. Never.'

Suddenly the band stops. The players step back a little, making room for their jovial, rotund leader, who bends his head to the microphone.

'Ladies, gentlemen, team members, it gives me very great pleasure to invite a special guest to sing for us tonight. This person is already a star in his own right, and as such is known to many of you. To others he will be strange. But he has agreed to sing for us, and it is my honour, not to mention my privilege, to welcome him to the microphone. Ladies and gentlemen, I give you' – there is a drum roll from behind him – 'our minister for sport, culture and youthful affairs, the Right Honourable George Ban-uba!'

Together, Rob and I spin around. Sure enough, the minister is on his feet and beaming. He walks down through the applauding crowd and up to the microphone. Detaching it deftly from its stand, he comes forward.

'Fellow countrymen and women, I would like to sing a bracket of songs for you, starting with a personal favourite.' He turns to the guitarist, makes counting-down movements with his head, swings back to the audience. 'Aha la Bamba la Bamba ...'

The audience explode like fireworks, jumping, squealing, grabbing partners, clapping, singing, dancing snapping their fingers. Rob is yelling and clapping, even Joyce is jumping. The audience won't let the minister go. He sings Elvis, Stevie Wonder, Abba, the Beatles, Harry Belafonte – nothing seems beyond his repertoire – while his team rocks and rolls and boogies and sings. I decide that if the Papua New Guineans show this amount of commitment on the sports field, they will be unbeatable.

Having saved money by staying in the Keleti Beach dormitory, I decide to treat myself to a proper hotel in town for a couple of nights. Bill runs me into Nuku'alofa in the resort van. 'Do you think you'll stay long in Tonga?' I ask him as we trundle along. He pauses for some time before replying.

'Maybe. I don't mind it myself, but Joyce ... She's not that keen on the place, y'know?'

As Bill drops me off in Vuna Road, his shoulders sag low, a cigarette still clings to his lower lip. I thank him, shake his hand, tell him how much I've enjoyed my stay at Keleti Beach. He smiles, wearily and a little sceptically.

'Good luck with your book,' he says.

'Thanks. Oh, the fare for bringing me here? How much?'

He waves his hand dismissively, then stops, frowns. 'Joyce didn't ask you fer the fare when you checked out?'

'No.'

He exhales sadly. 'She'll be expecting me to bring it, then.' His body seems to deflate even more as he looks up at me apologetically. 'That'll be ... ten puh-ung-ga.'

The next day I watch 35,000 people take to the streets of Nuku'alofa. Officially the walk is to celebrate Emancipation Day, but it doubles as a walk for Jesus because, in the words of King Tupou IV, 'King Tupou I was a born-again Christian in 1862 and that was the reason he granted freedom to the people at the time.' Tupou I, the present king's great-grandfather, was the founder of modern Tonga. Uniquely among South Pacific Island nations, Tonga does not celebrate an independence day, because it alone was never colonised, never ruled by a European power. This is a source of great pride to the nation of 100,000.

Nevertheless, the missionaries did a grand job of colonising Tonga. As in neighbouring Samoa, there are churches everywhere, not just those built by the original proselytisers, the Methodists and the Roman Catholics, but also those built later by the Church of the Latter Day Saints, the Seventh Day Adventists and the Jehovah's Witnesses. Judging by the newness and number of their churches, it's the well-heeled Mormons who are winning the race for Tongan souls.

I book into the town's best-known hotel, the International Dateline. It's a world away from Keleti Beach: big, sprawling and sleepy, located right on the waterfront and a five-minute walk from the town's main street. The hotel's logo is a sketch of the building with a vertical line – the international dateline – kinking around it to the right. In the lobby I find myself staring at the floor, because built into the marble is a large bas-relief of Tongatapu, and that kinked line again, in brass. The line is the reason Tonga subtitles itself 'The Land Where Time Begins'.

Back in the 1870s, when the European colonisers were trying to sort out a way of regulating an increasingly mobile world into time zones, an American academic came up with a system whereby the 360 degrees of the globe could be divided into twenty-four zones, each about 15 degrees of longitude apart, and each one hour behind the other, with Greenwich, London, being the prime meridian. In 1884 this sensible suggestion was accepted universally. There was only one snag: some small Pacific Island groups close to Greenwich's ante-meridian of 180 degrees – Fiji, Samoa and Tonga – were bisected by lines of longitude and would therefore suffer the inconvenience of having two different days of the week on some of their islands. Something pragmatic had to happen, and the logical solution was to make the 180-degree of longitude kink around these islands. But which way to kink? East or west?

In 1879 the colonial governor of Fiji decreed that the dateline should take a big kink east, incorporating all the islands of Fiji and Tonga west of the line, and giving them for all time the same day as New Zealand and Australia. The King of Samoa, however, went along with United States' demands that his islands be a day behind. And so it is possible, for those titillated by such matters, to stand on Tonga's easternmost island, Tafahi, on, say, a Monday, and look across to not very distant Savai'i, in Samoa, where it is the same time, except that it is Sunday. Luxury cruise ships clustered in this stretch of the Pacific Ocean celebrated the advent of the new millennium in Tongan waters on 31 December 1999, then sailed east the next day for an hour or so into Samoan seas and partied all over again, thus getting two millennium knees-ups for the price of one.

Tonga may be The Land Where Time Begins, but it is also The Land Where Time Appears to Stand Still. Nothing, but nothing, is done in a hurry. Although this maddens Palagis like Joyce, as I cycle around Nuku'alofa I think it's rather nice. Even rush hour is a relative term, with hundreds of well-used Japanese cars, some held together with rope and duct tape, creeping through the dusty, pitted streets. The road toll in Tonga must be very low. All transactions, from buying a banana in the market to reconfirming an onward flight, are done in slow motion. And just to make sure that nothing speeds up too dangerously, most dockets are still written by hand and carbon-copied.

Next day I leave for a day tour of Tongatapu with Lani, a very pleasant young woman from the Tonga Visitors' Bureau. The island is almost level, tilted a little to the north, and shaped like the slipper of a medieval knave. Nuku'alofa is located where the knave's laces would be tied. Although it appears at first inspection rather featureless, Tongatapu holds subtle secrets. At the eastern end of the island there are marvellous Maya-like tombs of Tonga's feudal kings, and the Trilithon, a prehistoric monument on a scale with Stonehenge and of equal significance. It is thought that the alignment of its massive menhirs was connected with the seasonal solstices, a knowledge vital for planting food crops such as taro.

In the evening, Lani takes me to the Tongan National Centre, a line of large fales built in traditional style and housing exhibition centres, a museum, handicraft workshops and display halls. Tonight there's Tongan dancing, a feast and a kava ceremony. The ceremony is carried out according to strict etiquette: the pepper tree root is beaten, mixed with water in a large carved bowl, strained through coconut fibre, then served to guests from a half coconut shell by a Tongan maiden. An honorary 'noble' is sought from the audience to take part in the performance, and a young Swedish man with long flaxen hair jumps up to volunteer. Afterwards he is presented with a certificate acknowledging this role, and I imagine him later trying to explain the significance of the kava ceremony to puzzled friends back in Göteborg.

'What does kava taste like?' I ask Lani.

She shrugs. 'I don't know, I've never tasted it. In Tonga, women can't drink kava, they just serve it to the men.'

The women get stuck with making tapa cloth, surely one of the most tedious and mind-numbing pastimes in the world, involving beating hibiscus bark with mallets, soaking it, beating it some more, and so on, for day after day after day, even before the painting of the patterns begins. By having exclusive rights to the kava drinking, men have got by far the best part of the cultural deal.

And they drink a lot of kava. There are 'kava clubs' everywhere. The churches don't disapprove of this, on the theory that if the men are filling themselves up with kava, which has a mellowing effect, they won't drink excessive amounts of alcohol and do damage to themselves and others. When later I taste some myself, I'm puzzled as to the liquid's appeal. It tastes like dishwater with some mud mixed in, and turns the lips numb. But drunk ceremoniously, with a group of other men, it's undeniably sociable.

'Don't Worry, Be Ha'apai', enjoin T-shirts all over Pangai, on Lifuka island. Pangai is the only town in the Ha'apai Group, a cluster of sixty-two beautiful atolls and volcanic islands, half an hour's flight from Tongatapu. And the timing of my arrival here is fortuitous because it's festival week, when most of

Ha'apai's population of 10,000 celebrate with sport, dancing, singing, parading, crafting and tug-of-warring. Ha'apai's festival is the foreplay that leads up to the big festival of Helaila, held on Tongatapu in the first week of July. This also celebrates the birthday of King Taufa'ahau.

I've arrived just in time for the tail-end of the festivities – the announcement of the winner of the Miss Ha'apai contest. First, though, there's the Crown Prince's cocktail party, to which someone has wangled me an invitation. The party is held inside a military compound on the Pangai waterfront. The venue itself is enclosed by barbed wire, but inside it's all very jolly as we stand under the stars and drink our Royal beer. Like all crown princes, His Royal Highness – the title's apt, since he also owns the brewery – attracts a great deal of gossip and notoriety. Educated at King's College, Auckland, and Sandhurst, the heir to the throne of Tupou is still unmarried. Known to have a predilection for girls from commoner ranks, he can nevertheless marry only into Tonga's nobility. Furthermore, affairs of state seem to very much bore HRH, as he is commonly known, and he spends much time flitting off to other lands. He even has that middleclass English affectation, a lisp. However, tonight on Ha'apai the Crown Prince appears to be on his best behaviour. His princely duties include dancing with all six finalists at the ball that follows the beauty contest.

Beauty pageants may now be *de trop* in many countries, but in the South Pacific they are still big-time. The Miss Ha'apai contest final is being held in the Toluafe Hall, just outside Pangai town, and I hitch a ride there with a young

American Peace Corps worker, John from Philadephia, on the back of a battered utility truck. The two of us are waved inside and immediately shown to the line of VIP seats at the front, just behind the Prince's throne, the governor's chair and the seats of the sponsors. This is embarrassing. Why should I be sitting up here? John from Philadephia explains, 'You're a visitor and a Palagi. The Tongans would consider it grossly ill-mannered for you to sit with the commoners.' So, to avoid offending my hosts, I remain at the front on my white plastic chair.

While we wait for HRH to make his appearance, some middle-aged women get up and do tau'olunga – solo dances – which are well received by the audience, then we wait some more. The hall is crammed with spectators. Above the stage are the banners of the festival sponsors, local businesses and Royal Tongan Airlines. The biggest and brightest banner is that of Benson and Hedges, its slogan, 'Turn to Gold', a message of unconscious irony, given that is the colour most users' lungs will turn if they continue to smoke at the rate they do. The international tobacco companies push their product shamelessly in Tonga, and with no restrictions on advertising and a cheap packet price, it's unsurprising that most men (but not many women) smoke.

The prince enters, using a walking stick for assistance (he suffers from gout), and wearing the faintly disdainful expression of a man who for a very long time has had everything he ever wanted. He takes his throne, there are many speeches, then the contestants come on. They wear elaborate ball gowns and most look petrified. They bow low to HRH, crimp their way down the catwalk and back, then exit. Only one looks relaxed, the very pretty and pert Miss Ha'apai Hardware, who prances, waves, and even gives HRH a cheeky grin. At this stage I decide to excuse myself. I can't take any more and, besides, I'm awash with Royal beer. As I walk out into the darkness, I stop and gape. Outside a wire fence, trying to peer in the windows, jostling each other for a better view, are several thousand people.

Later I hear that the winner of the beauty contest is Miss New Zealand-Ha'apai. I'm disappointed: I had hoped it would be bold little Miss Hardware.

Walking back through the town is like being blindfolded. There are no street lights, no house lights, no vehicle lights and no moon. I literally grope my way along the street, heading in what I hope is the direction of my hotel. Suddenly, from out of the darkness to my right, two massive figures loom over me. I think they are young men. Very large young men.

'Where you goin'?' The tone is challenging, aggressive. 'Yeah, man, where you goin'?'

I'm terrified. It's the first time I've ever been threatened on a Pacific island, and there's no one, absolutely no one, to help me. They're all back at the hall watching the beauty contest.

'You hear me, man? I said, where you goin'?' The tone is menacing now.

The two enormous figures come closer. I can see what I fear are bunched fists, and can hear their thick breathing. Swallowing with fright, I think as quickly as I can, then call out airily and in what I hope passes for a Utah accent, 'I'm on my way to church. The night service. I'm a Mormon missionary.'

A pause, then, 'Yeah? Where's your bro? Youse always goes in twos.'

'He's ... ah ... meeting the bishop.'

'The bishop?'

'Yes.'

There is silence for a few seconds. Then the two figures move aside, melting into the blackness of the night.

The Niu'akalo Beach Hotel is a kilometre up the coast from Pangai town, just past a statue of Shirley Baker and right beside the lagoon. Eight two-bedroom fales are set in a large well-tended garden which runs down to a sandy shore and the lagoon. Meals are taken in a small dining room on the covered patio facing the sea. There's a bar in the lounge and the whole place is small enough for the guests to get to know one another easily. Such intimate circumstances can be disastrous – one bore in the house could wreck an entire stay – but luckily this is not the case during my visit. I find myself in the company of a Danish couple, Henrik and Pia from Elsinore; Godfred, a Tanzanian engineer who designs harbours; and Irene, a Tongan-born woman who's returning to Ha'apai, after thirty years away, to trace her family's roots. Dining and drinking together, we're soon a small, jolly team. Although hailing from Hamlet's home town, Henrik is far from melancholic, and the lovely Pia shows no signs of dementia. Godfred is witty and articulate, and Irene has the natural dignity and courtesy of many Polynesian matriarchs.

Now that Ha'apai's festival is over, Pangai has subsided into a dusty torpor, so we spend most of our time sitting on the hotel patio with other visitors – the Niu'akalo is a popular gathering place for locals – talking about what we've found in Tonga, or just staring across the lawn, past the palms and at the skyline. There are several reasons why this is not an entirely idle pastime, for precisely where we are, and in the immediate proximity, are some of the most significant sites not merely in the Pacific but on Earth.

Just a few kilometres behind us is the Tonga Trench, a submarine chasm where the ocean plunges to unimaginable depths as the Pacific tectonic plate slides under its neighbouring Indo-Australia plate. This slow, inexorable collision has tossed up a line of live volcanoes, two of which, Tofua and Kao, we can look straight out at. And it explains why at least once a month these islands are heaved from side to side by seismic convulsions.

Kao – the highest peak in all of Tonga – is a perfectly symmetrical cone over 1,000 metres high. Neighbouring Tofua has decapitated itself through successive eruptions and now presents a low, smouldering profile on the horizon. Within the crater of Tofua is a large freshwater lake. It was while standing off this island, in April 1789, that Fletcher Christian seized the *Bounty* and cast William Bligh and eighteen others adrift in an open boat. Bligh sought food and water on Tofua, but did not scale its slopes and find the lake. The locals attacked the Englishmen, one of Bligh's men was killed and the party scrambled away to their boat. Later, while sailing between Viti Levu and Vanua Levu, they narrowly escaped being captured and eaten by a Fijian war party. They made no other landfall until they reached Timor, six weeks and 5,800 kilometres later. Today you can fly out to Tofua from Ha'apai in a float plane, land on the crater lake and eat a picnic lunch on its shore.

There is plenty of other human history in the vicinity. James Cook anchored *Resolution* and *Discovery* here in 1777, and the locals put on such a party for him and his crews that he named Tonga 'The Friendly Isles'. What he didn't know was that his host, a Machiavellian chief called Finau, was softening the Englishmen up in order to murder them and seize their ships. The plot was lost after a disagreement among the Tongans over the timing of the attack, and the English ships sailed away, for ever impressed by Ha'apaian hospitality.

Thirty years later, in 1807, Finau did manage to seize an English privateer, the *Port-au-Prince*, kill most of its crew and successfully employ its armaments against the defenders of Tongatapu. One of the English crew who was spared, Will Mariner, lived among the Tongans for several years before returning to England and writing a classic chronicle of his adventures, *An Account Of The Natives Of The Tonga Islands* (1817). The *Port-au-Prince* was beached just a bike-ride along from where we sit and watch the sun go down over Tofua and Kao, turning the sky the colour of marmalade.

On my second-to-last day on Ha'apai, a Sunday, I walk the three kilometres up the road to where the *Port-au-Prince* came ashore, and try to imagine the scenes that happened that day. It's difficult, as it's a place of utter serenity. Trudging back along the road in the early afternoon sun, I hear the soft *parp* of a car horn. A battered red Mazda draws up alongside me, and a youngish Tongan woman leans out the driver's window. 'You like a ride?' she asks, smiling in a slightly lopsided way. Alongside her is a grinning man in shorts, jandals and a blue singlet with the familiar 'Don't Worry, Be Ha'apai' slogan. 'Thank you,' I reply. It's thirty degrees on the road, and I flop gratefully on to the worn back seat.

'Like a trink?' The man in the front turns and passes over a 1125ml bottle of dark rum. It's half empty.

'Ah, no thanks. It's a bit early for me.'

'Cake?' He holds up a fat sponge cake on a cardboard plate. Several wedges are missing.

I take a piece. It's sweet, thick and gooey.

'Sure you doan wan a trink?'

'Quite sure, thanks.'

The man swigs happily from the bottle, then passes it over to the driver. She takes the bottle in one hand, takes a swig, hands it back and takes a wedge of cake. The man starts crooning an island song and she joins in. We drive contentedly on, along the hot, empty road.

'Where are you going?' I ask. 'To a party?'

The man burps. 'No. We already got a party. Here. Ha-ha-ha!'

'Dah-dah-dah-dah,' croons the woman. 'We drive round the island, having a party,' she giggles. 'Just him and me.' The car veers to the left and she corrects it hurriedly. 'Better than bloody church.'

Then I understand. It's Sunday, when nothing at all is sanctioned by the authorities except worship, and more worship. Eating between services is the only permissible pleasure. And now that the carnival is over, there's nothing to do on Ha'apai. *Nothing*. You're not even allowed to go fishing on the sabbath, let alone drink. No planes can take off or land, no shops are open, no secular activities are permitted. As one Tongan wag told me, 'If we were allowed to skydive on Sunday, even the parachutes wouldn't open.' My new friends' solution is a mobile, secret party for two, in the front seat of a Mazda. I applaud their initiative, and courage. The hotel approaches.

'Just let me out here, please.'

'By the ho-tel?'

'Yes please.'

The car skids to a halt, and the woman turns and grins. She seems deliriously happy. 'More cake?'

'No thanks. And thanks very much for the lift. It was a big help.'

'No worries, mate,' says the man, raising the rum bottle. It's now only a third full.

I get out and bend down to the driver's window. The woman gives me a dopey grin. 'Bye,' she drawls, rippling her fingers.

'Bye. Drive carefully.'

She giggles, puts the Mazda into gear, and they drive off slowly, both singing. The car weaves, but there's little danger of her hitting anything, because it's the only vehicle in sight.

By happy coincidence Henrik, Pia, Godfred, Irene and I are all on the same flight north to Vava'u. Before we leave, the

Royal Tongan Airlines people weigh not only our bags but us. One by one we step on to the scales and our body weights are carefully noted. The flight itself takes about forty minutes. Half an hour into the air and we're all exclaiming at the beauty of the islands of Vava'u, scattered across the ocean below us.

Vava'u is like a big piece of geological jigsaw puzzle, tilted south so that the sea has flooded its coast, turning valleys into sounds and mountains to hills. The result is a labyrinth of waterways, and ridges covered with rain forests and palm trees. And in the centre of these sounds, enclosed by hills, is the South Pacific islands' finest harbour, Port of Refuge.

It was the Spaniard Antonio Mourelle who, in 1781, came across Vava'u and the harbour at its core, joyfully naming it Puerto de Refugio. But the Tongans had been using it for about 3,000 years before that, calling it Lolo 'a Halaevalu, meaning Oil of the Princess Halaevalu, because of the sheen of the harbour's waters on a still day. Mourelle claimed the islands for Spain but nothing came of that, and today the harbour is treasured as a haven by hundreds of yachties from all over the world, who sail into it gratefully and moor right on the front step of the island's town, Neiafu. Yacht charters are big in Neiafu, too. As a result, the attractive hillside town contains an odd mix of people: Tongans in traditional tupeni (skirts), ta'ovalu (waist mats) and sandals wander about the streets, along with chic Californian couples in designer nautical gear, stocking up on their vegies, canned drinks, Chinese sneakers and handicrafts.

In Neiafu I'm staying at a newish hotel right above the

harbour. It's a heavy concrete-block building with a super-market on the floor above and a restaurant below the guest-rooms. Remembering the seismic hyperactivity throughout these islands, I scrutinise the block walls for possible fissures and wonder about local building codes, until I'm distracted by the panoramic view of yachts, harbour, hills and forest from the balcony. My travelling companions have dispersed to other parts of the town, but we're reuniting for dinner tomorrow night. After watching the twilight turn the coconut palms on the hills to mop-topped silhouettes, I go downstairs to watch television.

Back in Nuku'alofa the television stations serve up a mixture of cartoons, rabid evangelists from the American South, CNN news, and sport, mainly boxing and wrestling. Here in the far north, however, they haven't yet got live TV, although they're working on it. There is a satellite dish on the front lawn of the hotel. A big flex runs from it across the grass and through the bar window to the TV set, which is sitting on the bar. That this is a temporary arrangement can be deduced from the ditch that has been dug across the lawn, in readiness for the cable. Keen to see what has been happening in the world outside the kingdom, I watch a tall, pale, skinny American missionary who is fiddling with the TV's remote. He is getting jumpier by the minute and resorting to some very un-missionary language. Jamming his thumb on the remote button, he produces a picture of a very black, frizzy-haired woman extolling a brand of washing powder called, oddly, Omo. The missionary starts yelling. 'What the fuck is going on here? Where the fuck has CNN gone? Jesus ...'

It seems that the dish outside has been aimed at the wrong satellite, so that all we can get is a broadcast from Papua New Guinea. This consists mostly of Melanesians advertising cigarettes, deodorants and Omo, interspersed with old American comedy shows. This rapidly palls, so I go upstairs and get into bed.

Some time in the night I'm woken by a strange sensation. The room is swaying. Nothing sudden, nothing violent, it's just as if the building is swinging gently to a silent subterranean tune. The ceiling light swings back and forth, as if it's conducting the Earth's movement. Unmistakably, it is an earthquake. I lie paralysed, my mind convulsing in time to the movement of the tectonic plate. I think of the supermarket above, and the crammed shelves of canned beef and mackerel, jandals, Coke and Pepsi, Royal beer, cheeseballs and Chinese sneakers, under which I will be entombed, until my remains are dug out and displayed around the world on CNN news. But nothing happens. The swaying eventually stops and the building remains intact.

Next day, when I mention the incident excitedly to some locals, they shrug. Earthquake? Don't worry about it, they happen all the time. Later, back in Auckland, I see on *The New Zealand Herald*'s back page a dramatic aerial colour photograph of a newly born volcano which exploded out of the sea in western Vava'u the night I experienced the earthquake. The Tongans have to think up a name for the new island, but before they've settled on one there's another earthquake which takes the island back under the sea again.

As elsewhere in the South Pacific, on Vava'u the Church

of the Latter Day Saints seems to be winning the competition for local souls. But judging by one of the Mormon churches I see in Neiafu, the other faiths may be fighting back. Someone – an enraged Methodist, perhaps? – has torn some of the lettering from a cream painted wall so that it reads CHURCH OF THE LATTER DAY A NTS. Watching a group of identically clad Mormons slowly making their way up the street in the distance, it seems to me a particularly inventive piece of vandalism.

It is, I find, an illusion that time stands still in Tonga. As elsewhere, it flees. Godfred, Henrik, Pia, Irene and I have a farewell dinner in Neiafu – a Madras curry cooked by a Cockney. We exchange email addresses and hope we'll meet again. Henrik and Pia have met other Danes and are off to Suva to crew on their yacht, before returning to Denmark to breed. Irene is still finding family and Godfred has another wharf to design. We have had one of those travelling friendships, fleeting, fraternal, memorable. And as for Vava'u, well it's undeniably the loveliest part of Tonga. Yet recently young men in a rugby team from these islands went on a tour of New Zealand and, on the day they were due to fly home, vanished into the suburbs of south Auckland. It appears the rugby was just a pretext for the players to emigrate illegally. When it came to a choice of whether to spend the rest of their lives on beautiful tropical islands or take their chances on the mean streets of south Auckland, they made a dash for the latter.

A while ago, too, I had a fax from a schoolteacher at one of the secondary colleges on Vava'u. Her seventh form English class had been studying my South Pacific novel *Temptation*

Island as their set text, and had prepared some questions for me to answer. While flattered in the way authors always are by such requests, I was also surprised: the novel is about a South Pacific island whose government is corrupt, malfeasance is rampant, aid money squandered, the civil service bloated and press freedom severely curtailed. There is violence and more than a little sex in the story. It could be seen as subversive to place such a book in the hands of young Tongans, but bravely, in my opinion, the teacher had decided that it was important to do so. I faxed my replies back to the students but never heard from them or the teacher again. Then, just a few months later, a tropical cyclone struck Vava'u. The college had its roof blown off, causing, according to news reports, 'serious loss of school textbooks and other equipment'. To date I have not received any re-orders.

SEVEN

SURVIVING THE ROCK
NIUE

MILLIONS OF YEARS AGO a crustal convulsion beneath the Pacific Ocean heaved a huge coral atoll and its lagoon sixty metres above the sea. In time the coral fossilised into limestone, and its surface weathered into a veneer of soil which supported tropical bush and rain forest. About 1,800 years ago people from Tonga and Samoa discovered the big uplifted rock, named it and settled it, adapting skilfully to its singular topography, living by fishing and farming.

Captain James Cook and his crew sighted Niue's rugged shores on 20 June 1774, during the explorer's second world voyage. The next day Cook took possession of the island for Britain, somewhat unconvincingly, for on the three occasions he tried to land, coral rocks and small-arms fire were exchanged, obliging the Englishmen to sail away, although the explorer fixed the island's position nicely. Cook had his revenge on the locals by naming Niue 'Savage Island', a name which to this day rankles with Niueans everywhere – almost as much as it rankles when people confuse Niue with Nauru, a ravaged heap of bird excrement 3,000 kilometres away to the north-west.

Sailing away to the west, Cook noted of Niue, 'To judge the whole garment by the skirts it cannot produce much, for so much as we saw of it consisted wholly of coral rocks all overrun with trees shrubs etc and not a bit of soil was to be seen.' He then speculated on how the coral rocks, first formed in the sea, came to be thrown up to such a height: a pertinent question which had to await the following century and the new science of geology for a definitive answer.

In the 1840s the English missionaries arrived, and with the assistance of a Niuean convert, Peniamina, christianised the island. Niue chiefs gained British protection in 1900, and in 1901 Niue was annexed to New Zealand. The island achieved self-government in 1974, in free association with New Zealand. The most significant implication of this was that Niueans had open access to the country 2,200 kilometres to the south-west.

Niue is like a big, diamond-shaped dish raised above the ocean, in the centre of a triangle formed by Samoa, Tonga and Rarotonga. It is a rough diamond too, its cliffs battered and undercut by the sea, its ancient coral pinnacles scalpel sharp, its coastline and skirting reef providing no still-water anchorage. There is no surface water – no streams, rivers or lakes – and droughts are not uncommon. The island absorbs the tropical rainfall like a giant sponge, so the main water supply must be obtained through artesian bores.

How does an isolated, fossilised coral island with limited

natural resources generate enough export income to pay for the imports on which its population depends? This fundamental economic question is one faced by many Pacific islands. Some, such as Pitcairn, for a while went the postage-stamp way, but email and declining numbers of stamp collectors all but ended that. Tonga rents its airspace lucratively to American satellite companies, although most of the profits from 'Tongasat' go to the king's only daughter, Princess Pilolevu Tuita, who is rumoured to own 60 percent of the company. Tuvalu exploits its internet code '.tv'. For years Niueans tried to earn an export income from their traditional occupation, agriculture – copra, coconuts, kumara, passionfruit, limes. Nothing really worked. The island's skeletal soil, periodic storms and droughts, fickle shipping and prohibitive airfreight costs meant that such schemes, as elsewhere on remote Pacific islands, usually ended in backbreak and heartbreak. One local entrepreneur even tried freezing and exporting the excellent dry-grown Niuean taro to New Zealand, but this scheme too came to grief because of poor distribution and marketing.

Emigration began in the 1950s and '60s and reached a peak in the following decade. Niueans, attracted by relatively high wages and overtime in the factories of Auckland, turned their backs on their bush gardens, left their villages and bought a one-way plane ticket to New Zealand. The main export of Niue became Niueans. Whole families flew south, then wrote back and encouraged others to uproot themselves. The contemporary population figures stand out as starkly as the coral pinnacles which surround Niue: fewer than 2,000 people still live on the 'Rock' (as the locals call it); 2,000 live in Sydney and 20,000 in New Zealand. Most of the latter are now New Zealand-born.

And as the people flew away, remittances from relatives who had emigrated and New Zealand aid money became the primary sources of income for Niue. Aid money from New Zealand to Niue was, in per capita terms, the highest to any Pacific country, and most of it went towards maintaining a bloated government bureaucracy. During the 1990s, however, aid was severely cut by the New Zealand government. Lay-offs of public servants began, and the Niueans were urged to get on and develop their private sector. Was there a private sector in a nation of fewer than 2,000 people? There was, but it faced formidable obstacles.

Niue is separated from its nearest neighbour, Tonga, by 500 kilometres of open ocean. Its soil is so thin and its bedrock so hard that a compressor and pneumatic drill are needed to dig a decent grave and bury the dead. Goods imported or exported by sea must be loaded or unloaded laboriously at the small, exposed wharf. Then there were the airline woes. A scheduled air link with the outside world is an isolated island's life-support system, but Niue's air links with its neighbours and with New Zealand have been tenuous. For two years in the late 1980s almost all air services to the island were suspended, meaning that the only regular way in or out was the once-a-week flight by small plane via American Samoa – a circuitous route which was an impediment to all but the most determined of travellers. Then, on 4 February 1990, the west coast of Niue was blitzed by Cyclone Ofa, which inflicted grievous damage on the island's food crops and one hotel. Even though the hotel was situated twenty-five metres above the sea, coral boulders were hurled at it at point-blank range, like mortar bombs.

As the jet does a low sweep over Niue, the raised atoll's geographical features stand out vividly: a notched coastline and close-in reef to the west; a jagged makatea of coral to the east; an expanse of rain forest and scrubby interior; an encircling road punctuated by a few tiny villages; and a small cliff-top capital town, Alofi. On the plane with me is the viceregal party from New Zealand. One of the quaint legacies of Niue's close political ties to New Zealand is that the governor-general of New Zealand is also the governor-general of Niue. This means that at some time during each New Zealand governor-general's term of office, he or she will pay an official visit to Niue and exchange assurances of goodwill. I have been fortunate enough to be invited, along with other guests, for the visit of the current incumbent who, among other duties, is to declare open a new hotel.

At the airport the white-suited governor-general is garlanded and welcomed with due ceremony by the Niue prime minister, his cabinet and other dignitaries, including Miss Niue, winner of the local beauty pageant, before the rest of us are collected and driven away to our accommodation — in my case, a motel to the north-west of the island.

Although Niue lacks the spectacular peaks of a high volcanic island, there are panoramic views of the Pacific almost all the way along the road, which encircles the island some thirty metres above the sea. And the road is a good one:

wide and well surfaced, undulating gently as it passes through stands of coconut palms, plantation plots and scrubland vegetation, following the island's perimeter, which was in pre-uplift times the rim of the former atoll. The centre of the island is bush-covered, but even here the old coral protrudes like harrows through the farmed plots of land. And all around the island, where the rim dips or plunges to the sea, the landforms are a wonder.

Rainfall permeating the coral rock forms a lens of fresh water metres underground. Around the edges of the island, at sea level, the water leaks out, sometimes forcefully, sculpting the rock into a karst landscape. The coastline is particularly spectacular near Avaiki, where I'm staying. A track from the plateau descends through a sloping cavern, before emerging on to the reef. The cave is festooned with stalagmites and stalactites, pale brown in colour, their ends dripping like old men's penises. On the cave walls and ceiling the rock is smooth and tactile, shaped into fantastic patterns. In places the stalagmites and stalactites have met, forming fluted columns of stone like petrified tree trunks, and at the base of the caverns are blue-green pools, part fresh, part saline, where tiny fluor-escent fish and sea urchins make their home. Slipping into one of the pools, I'm refreshed immediately, by sea water on one side and fresh water on the other. Underwater the visibility is utterly clear, unclouded by sand or silt – a snorkeller's heaven.

When I snorkel off the wharf near Alofi, I can see for nearly forty-five metres. Although I'm stuck near the surface like a fly on a ceiling, every detail of the sea bottom far below is visible, every rock, every reef fish, even the outline of a sunken boat. I can see canyons of coral rock and the sinuous movements of a small, white-nosed reef shark as it patrols the sea bed. Then, just 100 metres from the wharf, there is a sudden fall-off and the purple of the ocean's abyss. In parts of Niue you can stand on a cliff, cast a line just metres out and it will land in water over thirty metres deep. And for that reason the island's fishing is uniquely accessible.

Every man on Niue fishes – with a bamboo rod from the rocks, a net from an aluminium dinghy, or a prong-like device from a traditional canoe. The Niuean canoe – the vaka – is a small, light outrigger whose hull is hewn from the trunk of a moota tree and whose outrigger is made from a fou sapling. The canoes have to be small and light, as they're carried down the cliff on their owners' shoulders. They are kept in the many storm-proof caves which pock the coastal cliffs, and are launched at dusk. Bigger fishing vessels have to be launched from the wharf at Alofi, using a derrick.

After the swim I explore the rest of Niue's coastline by bike. The first thing I notice is that the driver of every vehicle coming the other way waves at me. It's a cheering gesture that reminds me of the New Zealand of my childhood, when everyone in small towns waved to others on the road. The second discovery is that the perimeter road, in defiance of the laws of physics, always seems to be going ever-so-slightly downhill. This, plus the road's fine surface, makes biking an effortless pleasure.

Everywhere in the dozen or so villages of Niue, there are empty houses – not derelict, because they were strongly built, with poured concrete walls and roofs of corrugated fibrolite – but windowless and silent, surrounded by rampant, drought-defying tropical grass and creeper. The houses resemble old-style bus shelters, standing in reproach of the passengers who have taken one-way tickets to the Auckland suburbs of Grey Lynn, Kingsland or Otara.

My destination is the village of Hakupu. I'm carrying a letter from two Kingsland-based Niuean sisters to their grandmother. I arrive in the village in the late morning. There are the usual empty houses, but others which are obviously still inhabited. Washing is spread out to dry on the grass, doors are open, but along the dusty limestone road which cuts through the village nothing moves. No radios can be heard, no children's cries. I knock on a couple of doors before coming to a house where there is a pareu-clad girl of about nineteen. When I show her the name on the envelope, she points to a driveway.

'Down there. The old school. She is down there.'

Every village used to have its own school. Another consequence of emigration is that the primary schools have now been amalgamated, and all the young children attend one school in Alofi, leaving a long, empty classroom block in every village. Hakupu's classroom block, though, is not quite empty. As I walk towards it across the playing field I see that one room is still occupied – by elderly women. I ask for the person whose name is on the envelope – Trixie Ikinepule – and she comes forward, a large, dark-faced woman with a welcoming smile. I hand her the letter, which she leaves unopened for the moment and beckons me into the room.

The women, mostly in their sixties, sit on the floor with

their backs against the walls. Mats and pillows in the centre of the room provide a resting place for several pre-school children who look at me inquisitively. The women continue their work, chatting and laughing among themselves. They are weaving baskets, hats, place-mats and bags, using strips of dried pandanus. Half-completed crafts are everywhere: a white hat with a still-frayed brim; a coiled, catherine-wheel place-mat with its palm-frond core protruding; a basket with its handles not yet woven into place. Niuean crafts are famous, and looking at the beautiful chequered patterns created by dyeing some of the pandanus black, the intricacy and symmetry of the designs, the care and finish of the weaving, it's not difficult to see why. It's clear too that although the work is labour intensive for the women, it's also sociable and relaxing.

Mrs Ikinepule explains that her group is finishing a consignment of hats for the women of Rarotonga, who recently sent them boxes of oranges. Hats for oranges. The Rarotongan women are getting the best of the exchange.

Back on my bike, I discover more natural wonders. In several places around the coast the emerging fresh water has eroded gashes, creating chasms with walls fifty metres high. The most spectacular of these is Togo chasm, on the island's wild east coast. It is reached after a level walk through a virgin rain forest of mahogany, chestnut, pandanus and banyan trees. The forest ends abruptly, giving way to a steeply sloping zone of coral pinnacles from which there are sweeping views of an ocean so blue it is almost purple. I pick my way through the pinnacles, which are so sharp they can lacerate the skin at a touch. The track plunges further, swings right, and I am at the chasm edge. From there a sturdy ladder takes me down a further nine metres to the floor of Togo chasm.

The floor is covered with coral sand of purest white, hurled there through a cave at the ocean end during tropical storms. The sand is as soft as talcum powder, and provides a nursery for a number of coconut palms which have taken root there. The surrounding walls are dark grey and perfectly perpendicular, over thirty metres high on the landward side, only a little less on the seaward, while the chasm itself is only a few metres across. Togo is like a secret chamber, utterly soundless and windless, a unique wonder of the Pacific.

Wandering up to the end of the ravine, I scramble over a heap of boulders. At this, the landward end, the chasm floor is covered with moss and the palms are more profuse. A few more metres on, the way is blocked by a pool of murky green water. The chasm tapers, and there is no way further in without special caving equipment. I return to the soft white sand, gaze again at the sheer rock walls, and think perversely what a magnificent place this would be for a candlelit dinner party. This impure notion is rapidly replaced by the refrain of an old song: 'Rock of ages, cleft for me'.

Biking west, through the village of Hakupu, I slow the bike, stop, rub my eyes. I must be hallucinating. No, I'm not. There are hundreds of llamas spread over the scrubby landscape, grazing contentedly. What are they doing here, on a raised atoll in the middle of the South Pacific? Without being an animal expert, I know llamas are native to South America, and South America is quite a long way from Niue.

I feel like the person in *Jurassic Park* who comes across a herd of foraging dinosaurs. Cycling up to a corral where there are about twenty females and baby llamas, some clustered in the shade of a spreading tree, others with their heads in a large concrete drinking trough, I dismount and lean on the fence. The babies are gorgeous, leggy and snub-nosed, the wool on their legs and necks white, their backs a ginger colour which matches the bare earth around the corral. The adults are uniformly pale ginger.

As I'm standing in the sun wondering about all this, a young woman in blue overalls, large sunglasses and a brown Aussie stockman's hat comes out of the hut next to the corral, carrying a baby llama in her arms. She sets it down on the ground and tells me that she is from Tonga, that she is a vet and that the llamas are on Niue for quarantine purposes. They're from Peru, where all good llamas come from, and they've flown to the island on a specially adapted jet plane. They spend some months on Niue, then they're flown to farms in Australia, where they're shorn. Llama wool is highly valued in the garment industry, and Niue receives a per head payment for the animals' stopover on the island.

Every other Saturday on Niue is inter-village cricket day. Matches are played on village greens, but that's where the resemblance between the English version of cricket and kilikiti begins and ends. Standing at one end of Alofi's uncut green, I try to make out exactly what's going on. For a start, there are many more than eleven fieldsmen and two batsmen – about thirty at a rough count, boys and young men in shorts, sneakers and T-shirts. Women, girls and very young children watch from palm-frond shelters at either end.

There are wickets, a pitch of sorts, two batsmen, yes, but their bats are like large, angular war clubs, and alongside each batsman are a number of other men carrying long whips. A few fieldsmen stand at the edge of the green, others are on the road, and some sit on the wall bordering the green.

A bowler lopes in, hurls down the ball. The batsman swings, connects with it on the full, lofts it high over an acacia tree beyond the green. Everyone whoops and claps as the men with the whips sprint to the other end, turn and run back. The ball is found and thrown to a bowler. It's a very hard ball, the Niue Special. Unlike the Samoan kilikiti ball, which is made from bound rubber, this is a lacrosse ball, imported from Canada, and it has the weight and density of iron. But the Niuean batsmen have superb hand-eye coordination: one smites a full toss right across the green, over the road, over the Alofi wharf and into the sea, precipitating cheers, shouts and prolonged hilarity from the spectators. A man in the outfield grabs a mask and flippers, puts them on and dives to the bottom of the sea to retrieve the ball.

I can't comprehend the rules, but it's clear that everyone's having a great time. A burst of frenetic belting of the ball, and whip-cracking charges between the wickets, is followed by long periods of idleness and chat. Perhaps it's not so different from the flannel-trousered Lords version, after all.

Towards mid-morning I leave the cricket, but I ride past the green a few more times that Saturday. The game continues all morning, all afternoon, and concludes only when darkness descends over the island. Later I ask one of the players – who had to be taken to the hospital to have the webbing in his right hand stitched after he stopped a crashing hit – who won the match. He looks perplexed at the question.

'Ah … I think we made about … 400 runs. And Hakupu made …' he shrugs. 'I don't know what they made. About the same.'

'So who won?'

'I don't know.' He grins. 'It doesn't matter. It was a good game.'

Many of the Niue locals have strong connections with New Zealand. Indeed, many of them are New Zealanders. Ernie Walsh is a Kiwi electrician who first came to the Rock in the 1950s, married a local woman, returned with her to Christchurch to raise their large family, then came back to the island with her in 1987 to retire. But Ernie has only semi-retired, because he has a five-metre aluminium boat, *Tuaki*, rigged for fishing. He's sharp-eyed, fit, and extremely knowledgeable about local conditions.

The derrick swings *Tuaki* out from Alofi's concrete wharf and lowers her gently into the water. It's nine o'clock on a nearly moonless Niuean night. Ernie starts up his 400hp Mariner outboard, manoeuvres the boat up to the wharf, and we climb aboard. There is a light atop a PVC stem on the prow of *Tuaki*; another glows from a stem on the stern. We cruise out through the inky sea and turn east. Conditions are good, with the cuticle moon shining weakly in the west. My Niuean friend, Faama, stands in the bow; I stand in the stern, braced against the railing. We both hold nets with three-metre-long handles which make them cumbersome but give us good reach. *Tuaki* rolls gently as we motor along the coast, under the cliffs. I peer at the water. What happens next?

Faama shouts from the bow. 'There!'

Looking left, I see a small fish skittering across the surface of the black water. It darts in one direction, then tacks back in another. Ernie swings the wheel to starboard but the fish has gone.

'Behind you!' Faama shouts, and I turn to see the fish zoom like a small missile towards the boat. I shove the net out clumsily, lunge at it, and hear a whoop of triumph from Faama and a chuckle from Ernie. By extraordinary good luck for me, and considerable ill-fortune for the flying fish, it has flown straight into my net. Hauling the net in, I grab the fish and drop it in a bucket, where it flops pathetically, wings flailing against the sides.

For the next two hours we cruise slowly along the coast, from time to time swiping and scooping at the creatures which leap, flutter and glide towards *Tuaki*'s light. Occasionally the fish leap at the light, land in the water and float inert, as if waiting to be scooped up. Others are more assertive. One launches itself from the water and flies straight at Faama's face. He ducks away just in time, and it swishes past him and back into the water on the other side of the boat.

Fly fishing, as it's called, is a combination of lepidoptery, whitebaiting and small-game hunting. It's also hilarious, at least for those on board, although more than half of the fish that come for our light manage to evade the nets. Even the ones which stun themselves by striking our gunwales usually sink immediately.

There are also sea snakes everywhere. They lie ribbonlike on top of the water, twisted into S shapes, unafraid of humans. Understandably, this part of Niue's coast is known as Snake Gully. The creatures call to mind Coleridge's lines:

Within the shadow of the ship
I watched their rich attire:
They coiled and swam; and every track ...
Was a flash of golden fire.

These ones are banded, usually yellow and black, and venomous, although their mouths are so small they find it difficult to get a grip on a human. The skin between the fingers is something they can get their teeth into, Faama tells me.

Curious, I scoop up a couple in my net, but they slip through the mesh. Then Faama nets a bigger one, pulls it aboard and drops it into the bucket. It convulses, writhes its way up and out, and slithers across the bottom of the boat towards me. I have seldom seen anything so repulsive, and I'm about to leap overboard when I remember that there are many more out there in the water waiting, so instead I jump up on to the gunwale until Faama, laughing helplessly, snatches up the snake and throws it back in the sea.

At half-past eleven, with sixteen flying fish in the bucket, we draw up alongside the wharf. Ernie's wife Hine is there with the tractor. *Tuaki* is hooked up to the derrick, Hine drives the tractor off a few metres and the boat is hoisted from the water and lowered on to her trailer. It's quicker than using a boat ramp, and besides, there is no ramp, even on this, the sheltered side of the island, because of the persistent swell.

Under the wharf light I examine the catch. Flying fish are shaped like big herrings, though they have much larger eyes and their skin is slimier – to assist, I assume, their egress from the water. Their strong tail is used to break the tension between water and air; the large, delicate, folding wings are used for gliding, and can keep them airborne for fifty metres or so. They're good eating, if rather bony, but Ernie takes this catch to use as bait for larger prey the next day.

At dawn we pull away from the wharf on *Tuaki* again. Ernie has rigged her with two rods, one on each gunwale, and two reel lines. Faama attaches lures to the reel lines and bait to the rod lines. The reels are made, with typical island ingenuity, from old motorbike hubs with handles welded to them, and they trail plastic lures about ten metres behind the boat. These are teasers for the main bait, the flying fish, which troll much further behind. The two dead fish are attached to traces attached to the rods, and inside the bait are concealed two large, lethal-looking double hooks.

As we roll slowly along Niue's western coast, the horizon turns apricot and a molten sun rises from the sea, turning the sky bright and clear apart from a trail of small grey clouds just above the horizon. To starboard, the island is a long, black, level expanse, like the profile of a slumbering whale. By the time we round the northern end of the island, daybreak is complete and the coastal features are very clear. The grey-brown cliffs are about twenty metres high, notched where fresh water has emerged at the foot of the water-table edge and neatly undercut by the sea. There is bush on the highest ground, the occasional canoe landing is visible, but there is no other sign of human settlement. It occurs to me that this, the 'skirt' of the island, is Niue just as Cook and his men first viewed it from *Resolution* in June 1774.

Now we are adjacent to the eastern coast, the windward side of the island. Although the trade wind is gentle today, the ocean swells are strong and the water occasionally turbulent as current and tide conflict. *Tuaki* rolls on, the lures and baits tumbling in her wake. The sun is hot, the sky almost cloudless. Although we remain fishless, it's an uncommonly pleasant way to start a day. And we have company in the form of the little vaka – outrigger canoes – which bob about on the ocean. They're so insubstantial that from a distance it appears the fishermen are sitting on the sea, and I wonder how they manage when the weather is less clement.

Faama says, 'Most of those guys can't swim, so if they fall out they're in trouble. But they keep an eye on each other and help out in all kinds of ways. If one hooks a marlin, for example, the others will see it broach and come over and help get it in. The one who's hooked it wraps the line around his thigh as a brake.'

'A nylon line, around his thigh, with a marlin at the other end?'

'Right. You look at a Niuean man's leg. If he's a good fisherman, he'll have line scars across it. Sometimes they get towed all night by a big fish.'

With the sun climbing the sky and its rays burning our backs, Ernie turns the boat and we begin the long journey back. There have been no takers for our trailing morsels, it's after ten o'clock and the sun's too bright for big fish. Ernie points out landmarks on the cliff as we pass – a church wrecked by Cyclone Ofa and subsequently abandoned, a canoe landing place, the motel where I'm staying. He also explains that his family back in Christchurch will never come to Niue to live. The wages are much too low. 'The wife and I only get a quarter of the superannuation that we'd get back in New Zealand. That's why I do these fishing trips.' But he's clearly disconsolate. 'I hate taking out visitors and not getting a fish.'

'Well, that's the way it goes. It's good just to be out on the water.'

'Yeah, but I still hate not getting …'

'Hey! Hey, Ernie!'

The shout comes from Faama in the stern. Turning, I see that one rod's bent, its reel shrieking. Ernie shoves the boat into neutral, and as he does so the motorbike hub on the same side as the bent rod begins to spin. A double strike, and no time to get a harness on. I scramble aft, Faama takes the rod from its holder, hands it to me, barks orders.

'Reel in, reel in! Keep the tension on!'

Braced against the stern rail, rod butt digging into my groin, I obey. Whatever's on the other end is heavy, and fighting hard, but by applying all my energy I feel it yield. Minutes later I see flashes of electric blue and silver behind the boat, reel harder, and the fish is alongside. Faama gaffs it, hauls the flapping fish aboard, clubs it with a wooden truncheon and goes back to winding in the rodless line.

It's a wahoo, a long, tapering, blue-black fish with a pointed head, upright tail flukes and razor-sharp teeth. Blood leaks from its gills as it lies, dying. Faama winds in the second motorbike hub, a relatively simple operation, and hauls a second wahoo aboard. We must have passed through a school of them. We're all gleeful, and so I understand a possible derivation of the fish's name. It's so exciting to catch one that you can't help yelling, 'Wa-hoo!'

Returning to the wharf, we see the governor-general's party preparing to be taken out on a game fishing trip. But alas, His Excellency's boat returns hours later from its voyage along Niue's northern coast with no catch at all.

Every village on Niue has a church, a big church, sometimes an extremely big church. In Liku, a village whose population has been decimated by emigration, the church is nearly as long as the green next to it, although half the houses surrounding it are empty. It is built of concrete blocks, with stainless-steel guttering and long-run iron roofing – all imported from New Zealand. The cost must have been crippling.

Loveliest of Niue's churches is the one at Avatele, which is also the island's prettiest village. Located at the southeastern corner of Niue, Avatele has a huge green which slopes down from the church to the road. The church is large, white, steepled, but in need of a paint job. Women, all in woven hats, and men, mostly in dark suits, are ambling towards the church as I arrive. Avatele is providing lunch for the governor-general and his party, and the neighbouring community centre – a long, low building decorated with palm fronds – has tables and chairs set out under its verandah, awaiting the dignitaries' arrival. In the meantime, I attend the village church service.

A suited man greets me at the door and tells me, 'Sit anywhere you like.' This is easily done – although I'm a few minutes late, there are only six people scattered about on the wooden pews. I take a seat on the left-hand side, and wait. With its towering ceiling, the church is airy and not too hot. The high pulpit is flanked by two lower ones, and all three are decorated with vases of scarlet hibiscus flowers.

A youngish, skinny Palagi – European – woman comes in, looks around nervously and sits down next to me. She's wearing a floppy white sun-hat and a dark blue, floral-patterned dress. With her very thin, sharp features and stick legs, she looks like a pied stilt. As we wait for the service to begin, she tells me she's from Wellington and is staying in a village guest-house.

'What's it like?' I ask.

She looks doubtful. 'I can *see* the cockroaches, and deal with them. But this morning there were *teeth marks* in my pawpaw.' Then she brightens. 'But after this I'm going back to finish roasting the leg of lamb we brought from home. We're having roast carrots, roast potatoes and Surprise peas, too. And I'll do gravy and mint sauce. We brought all our food with us from Wellington, in a suitcase. It makes the holiday so much cheaper.'

Roast lamb and gravy? Even in mid-morning, inside the airy church, it must be going on thirty degrees.

The pastor enters through a side door, stands on high in the pulpit and, when he sits, disappears altogether behind the lectern. He's quite young, late twenties perhaps, with short crinkled hair, a flat face and blackcurrant eyes. The service alternates between Niuean and English, with most of the sermon devoted to giving thanks in various directions. A surprisingly adult Boys' and Girls' Brigade, who marched in at the beginning with banners, assist in these expressions of gratitude and frequently take up positions at the lower lecterns.

A collection is taken up during a hymn and the woman and I both put five dollars in the dish. The money is promptly counted by a man at a table in the front of the church, who writes figures in an exercise book, then delivers the book to the pastor, who at the conclusion of the hymn gives thanks, 'For the offerings made today, which total twenty-six dollars and eighty cents.'

The hymns are sung in rollicking fashion to the accompaniment of a synthesiser played by a tall, slim, greying man with a small moustache. Later I learn that he is Hima Takelesi, local musician, broadcaster and businessman, who is to become Niue's next high commissioner to New Zealand. The singing lacks the volume and part-harmony of Cook Islands' singing or the lustiness of Samoan congregations, but is still melodious enough to lull me into a very secular stupor.

There is a laid-back aspect to this service. People shuffle and scratch; a dog strolls in through the pastor's door and up the aisle without admonishment. The Boys' Brigade members don't bother to stifle their yawns: one goes to sleep and is woken up only when another one passes around a packet of cheeseballs. Babies in their grandmothers' arms goo, gurgle and eventually drop off to sleep too. My only discomfort is caused by the woman behind me, who has the worst case of halitosis I've ever smelt. Every time she holds a high note I'm engulfed by her breath, and even by shuffling a metre or so to the left I can't escape the fallout.

But by the time we stroll outside into the sunshine the air has cleared and I feel benevolent and reposeful, as if I've been meditating, which in a way I have. The stilt-legged woman walks off to baste her leg of lamb, a couple of elders shake my hand and thank me for coming, and that's it. There's another service after lunch, but I'll leave it to the locals. Sunday on Niue, as in Tonga, is high Victorian in its strictures: no shopping, fishing, working, or playing games. Swimming is tolerated, but only just. But I also get the impression that the church's primary function here is more social than spiritual, that the services, like the games of kilikiti, are a chance for the community to get together, talk and enjoy themselves.

Next day it's the lunch at Avatele for the governor-general of New Zealand and Niue and his party. His Excellency arrives in the New Zealand High Commission limousine, a long white vehicle which draws up and parks at the bottom of the expansive, sloping village green. He and his party walk up the hill to the community centre and take their seats at the long table under the verandah. Girls walk to and fro, waving palm fronds over the food to keep the flies away. There are prayers from local leaders, a song from the assembled, and the speeches begin. A village leader talks at length, then presents the governor-general with a gift: a beautifully carved and rigged model of a Niuean vaka. The governor-general makes a heartfelt and eloquent speech of reply, concluding with, 'And now, we have a gift for you, from the people of New Zealand.' Then he looks around expectantly at his aide-de-camp, and waits for the gift to be handed to him.

The aide-de-camp hesitates for a few moments, then goes over and whispers to the governor-general, who nods. The aide-de-camp walks off down the hill towards the car. 'Our gift will be here shortly,' the governor-general explains, then resumes speaking to the assembled gathering, this time extemporaneously. He is an excellent speaker, and the Niueans nod appreciatively as he says how moved he has been to visit their lovely island. But when a few minutes later the aide-de-camp returns, he is empty-handed. He whispers in the governor-general's ear, and the redness of his face is not entirely due to the midday heat. His Excellency, now also a little flushed, clears his throat and tells the crowded table, 'It seems that our gift is locked in the boot of the High Commission vehicle. The boot is being unlocked and the gift will be here shortly. In the meantime ...' The governor-general looks unusually wild-eyed for a moment, then looks down exultantly at his hosts. 'Why don't you ... *sing*!'

The Niueans look confused for a few seconds, then they too recover. Rising to their feet, they launch into a song, which sounds as if it could be a hymn. They sing one verse, then another, then sit down. The governor-general and his party applaud loudly, but there's no disguising the fact that we can all see the aide-de-camp working frantically at the boot of the limousine, and that it is still firmly shut. The governor-general rises once more – 'Your singing is wonderful. We would like to hear some more. Do sing for us again.'

A little uncertainly this time, the Niueans stand, then break hesitantly into song. Once they're away, their singing intensifies, their unaccompanied voices rising and falling beautifully before fading away some minutes later. As the Niueans sit down, the viceregal party applauds again, but the gift has still not been liberated from the boot. The governor-general launches into yet another speech, this one a little repetitive. He is obviously beginning to feel the strain. This is not how viceregal timetables are meant to proceed. The Niueans too are looking discomfited, probably because they know that their song repertoire has been exhausted. Then, just as it looks as if the event will have to be reorganised, the aide-de-camp arrives, breathless and flushed, bearing 'the gift from the New Zealand people to the people of Niue'. It is handed over with due ceremony, a speech of acceptance is made and, with relief, everyone sits down to lunch.

One of the most appealing aspects of any island is that it attracts eccentrics, people who have retreated from a large, densely populated land mass to a much more circumscribed world surrounded by sea, in the hope that their unconventional habits can remain intact. And to some extent that is true. I have met or observed many people on islands whose way of life would be the subject of ridicule elsewhere but is tolerated by fellow islanders.

I cannot imagine, for instance, the Italian environmental sculptor I once met in Samoa practising his art back in his native Milan. Gino went from lagoon-side village to lagoon-side village throughout Samoa, setting up trios of trimmed palm tree trunks in the sand, aligning them perfectly east to west. What was the purpose of this? To use the life-forces created by his sculptures to repair the hole in the ozone layer.

On Niue you don't have to look for long to find such people. Every evening, for example, just out of Alofi, a pair of swimsuited Americans, a man and a woman, come down to a small bay, carrying a kind of harness. They slip into a large rock pool, secure one end of the harness to the shore and the other to themselves, and swim. They swim and swim, steadily, diligently, one arm over, then the other, for an hour, staying in precisely the same spot. When this aquatic exercycling began some time ago, the locals would gather at the top of the steps leading to the rock pool and watch in wonder. Some of the children giggled, which upset the Americans, but now they are just part of the local scene. Rumour has it that the swimmers-who-go-nowhere are former flower children and acid-droppers who left not only their hearts but many of their brain cells in San Francisco.

There is also the usual impermanent population of yachties, moving through the Pacific before the cyclone season begins. Their boats are moored in Alofi Bay, and on their visits ashore they add a cosmopolitan flavour to the island. While I'm here the little flotilla includes some nautical Sloane Rangers (*very* English public school), some Germans, and Philippe and Heidi, from Switzerland, who make their presence felt almost immediately. He is about thirty-five, and very skinny, with an untidy beard and red pot-scourer hair, like Tom Hanks in the latter stages of the movie *Cast Away*. He goes around the island in shorts and bare feet. Heidi is very short, with blonde, Joan-of-Arc-style hair. She is about sixty. They have both been burnt dark brown by the Pacific sun.

Philippe grins and shouts at everyone as he passes. 'Hellaw! How are you! Ees fine day! Yes! Good day for swee-ming, for snark-ling, yes!' And always at his side is tiny, ageing Heidi, beaming a grin as wide as the island's horizon.

One morning at the wharf I see them loading a basket of coconuts into their inflatable tender, and call out greetings. Philippe grins dementedly, waves his arms around his head.

'Yes, yes, ees loverly day! Wonderful day! We get coconuts from market, see?'

Heidi nods, beams, points down at the laden basket.

'Where have you sailed from?' I ask them.

Philippe flings his arms in a roughly northerly direction. 'Med-dee-terr-ran-ean! Af-rica! West In-dies! Pun-a-mah! Tah-hee-tee! Rar-ro-tong-ga! And now ...' He looks around confusedly, as if seeking a signpost. 'And now ... we are ... *here*!'

'It's a long trip you're on, then.'

His eyes bulge further, he leans back, shouts again. 'Yes, yes, long long trip! Not over yet! Rest of world! New Zee-land! Os-tral-ya! May-lay-syuh! And ... others ... Very hard work!' He throws his arms about. 'We go now, to boat, with coco-nuts! Ees lovely day, yes!'

And the odd couple push off in their inflatable.

Biking along the road from my motel, I call in at another, newer motel at Avaiki, where friends are staying. I ask them if their accommodation is satisfactory. 'Oh yes,' replies Jane, 'it's lovely here.' Then she looks cross. 'Apart from the Germans next door.'

There are three middle-aged Germans in the next unit, Jane explains, two men and a woman, who make a lot of noise. Not raging parties or anything like that, but radio transmitting, most of the day and all of the night. They call Berlin, Munich, Hamburg on their powerful transmitter, and the sounds carry through the wall, especially in the still of night. Jane saw one of the Germans pay one of the Niueans who is working on the building site next to the motel five dollars to climb up the big coconut palm outside their unit with an aerial. He stuck it on the top, then climbed down again. The Niuean man told Jane that the Germans chose this motel especially: it was the only one with a very tall coconut palm right outside the door.

At first I think Jane must be exaggerating about the radio noise, but when I pass their unit on my way out, sure enough they are at it, headphones on, frowning with concentration, twiddling dials, speaking German into microphones. What on earth can be going on?

Back at my motel, I mention this odd behaviour to a man I've met here, David, who happens to be Jewish. He laughs, but with a degree of unease.

'Are you sure they're Germans?'

'Quite sure. They come from Bavaria, apparently.'

David's smile vanishes. 'Bavaria? Hitler had his power base there, didn't he?' He glances around, feigning anxiety. 'Could they be preparing for the new world order?'

Unable to resist this intrigue, I inquire further. Yes, most people have seen the Germans, but no one knows precisely why they're here. People just assume they're tourists. I get nowhere with my research until I ask Stafford Guest, expatriate Kiwi proprietor of Sails Restaurant, further along the road. He shrugs.

'The Germans? They're radio hams. Lots of them come here, the reception's so clear. No interference. And by sending their calling cards to Europe from such an obscure island, the cards become quite valuable. Collectors' items.'

'You can relax,' I tell David. 'They're just radio hams.'

David frowns, glances round. 'Radio hams? *The perfect cover ...*'

Leaving Niue, staring down at the island lying like a great green pancake in the sea, I wonder, can this rocky, isolated nation survive the economic gales which have in recent years battered it as severely as any tropical cyclone? Nobody can say for certain, but no island deserves to survive more, not only because it is a rare phenomenon of nature but because of the people who have remained there to help stem emigration and keep the country alive.

Later, continuing to monitor events on Niue from a distance, I learn that when the last of the llamas flew away they were not replaced. It was a scheme almost certainly defeated by economics. As a business, though, it made more sense than another short-lived scheme – the conversion in the late 1990s of the original Niue Hotel to a medical school. This plan, devised by some overseas opportunist, must have been the wackiest of all the get-rich-quick schemes to be foisted on a South Pacific island in recent times. Mercifully, and predictably, the medical school died. Who in the world would recognise a medical qualification from an island they'd never heard of?

But as Niue entered the new millennium, there were signs of fresh hope. Although the population had declined to around 1,700, and was continuing to fall, occupancy rates at the new Matavai Resort had improved. The island's air connection problems with the rest of the Pacific were finally sorted out when Polynesian Airlines started flying once a week direct to Niue from Auckland and back. Tourist numbers, although still modest, began to creep up, consisting mainly of people who wanted to dive, fish or explore the island's remarkable topography. An efficient infrastructure was installed, and the loony schemes were replaced by soundly based ones: a fish-processing plant and a vanilla-growing operation. Then, in one afternoon, on 6 January 2004, all was lost.

Cyclone Heta had walloped both Samoas and side-swiped Rarotonga before it struck Niue. On its way it had steadily gained in intensity. Its winds were gusting up to 275 kilometres per hour and Alofi was right in its path. For five hours – reaching a peak at 1.30 p.m. – the cyclone blasted the island, creating huge waves which surmounted the twenty-five-metre-high cliffs with ease and drove on inland, devastating buildings, crops and trees, and killing a young nurse. The hospital, museum, hotel, fuel-storage tanks, dive school, industrial enterprises and homes were totally wrecked. A sea surge forty metres above normal sea level coincided with the afternoon's high tide. When the sea receded, the coastline looked as if it had been struck by a small nuclear explosion. Alofi had virtually ceased to exist. It was Niue's worst calamity in living memory.

Niue was not just back to square one, it was back much further. Although aid was rushed in and generous international assistance offered, once again those remaining on the island were presented with two choices: fly away for good, or stay and start all over again. Does the world's largest raised atoll have a viable future? Only time, lots of time, and money, lots of money, will tell. The latest figure suggested for rebuilding Niue is twenty-five million New Zealand dollars. Twenty-five million dollars for 1,700 people.

EIGHT

HERMAN MELVILLE'S VALLEY
THE MARQUESAS

'**N**OTHING CAN EXCEED the imposing scenery of this bay. Viewed from our ship as she lay at anchor in the middle of the harbour, it presented the appearance of a vast natural amphitheatre in decay, and overgrown with vines, the deep glens that furrowed its sides appearing like enormous fissures caused by the ravages of time. Very often when lost in admiration at its beauty, I have experienced a pang of regret that a scene so enchanting should be hidden from the world in these remote seas, and seldom meet the eyes of devoted lovers of nature.'

The scene that so inspired Herman Melville was Taiohae Bay on the island of Nuku Hiva in the Marquesas Islands. In 1842, weary of the privations of shipboard existence on the whaler *Acushnet*, the twenty-three-year-old American jumped ship in the bay. Taking advantage of a tropical downpour to conceal his movements, he and another young deserter, Toby Greene, slipped away from the other sailors, who were sleeping in a canoe shed, and plunged into the tropical bushes which lay just beyond the beach. They made their way inland, through dense undergrowth, and along sheer-sided mountain ridges, and on the fourth day descended into the valley of the Taipivai people.

The valley was an imprudent destination, being home to a tribe whose ferocity was unparalleled, even by the standards of the Marquesas, where inter-valley warfare, tribal slaughter and cannibalism were endemic. 'Their very name is a frightful one,' Melville wrote later, 'for the word "Typee" in the Marquesan dialect signifies a lover of human flesh.' Each of the many deep valleys in the islands supported a large population who lived in fear and loathing of those in the other valleys. War clubs called u'u, carved from hardwood trees, were used in battle. Human sacrifice and cannibal feasts were part of the culture, and prisoners could expect nothing but violent death.

However, instead of being killed and eaten, Melville and Greene were seized and kept under a kind of house arrest for three and a half weeks, before being taken separately from the island by other sailing ships. Melville eventually made his way back to the United States, where he was legally discharged from sea service in 1843.

Melville's experiences in the South Seas, heavily embellished with romanticism and invention, were published as the novels *Typee* (1846), *Omoo* (1847) and *Moby Dick* (1851). *Moby Dick* was Melville's magnum opus, but *Typee* remains his most popular book. In the novel the young deserter discovers love with the Princess Fayaway in the valley of the Typee, extols the life of the Marquesan people and rails against the brutality of European intervention in their lives. Melville's writing is overwrought and didactic in the nineteenth-century manner, but through it shines his idealism, and his disgust at the way European 'civilisation' had shattered the lives of the indigenous people. And there was much to be disgusted about.

The twelve islands of the Marquesas, today part of French Polynesia, lie 1,200 kilometres north-east of Tahiti. An archipelago of volcanic monoliths, and further from a continental landmass than any other islands on Earth, they were first settled by Polynesian voyagers from the west – probably Samoa – about 2,000 years ago and became a dispersal centre for further migrations, to Hawaii, Easter Island, the widely scattered islands of southern Polynesia and, eventually, New Zealand. The Marquesan language is more akin to New Zealand Maori than to Tahitian.

Even today it is not difficult to imagine the exhilaration of those early discoverers when they first sighted the islands they called Te Hunua Enata, The Land of Man, for they are like no others in the South Pacific. Lying from seven to ten degrees south of the equator, their profiles are not softened by encircling white sands, nor is the force of the Pacific's waves kept at bay by barrier reefs or languid lagoons. Instead, the sides of the islands are perpendicular, plunging sheer to the floor of the ocean from which they erupted, millions of years ago, during a tectonic spasm. Ocean waves, driven by south-easterly trade winds, dash themselves against the basalt cliffs, but fortuitously there are many inlets and sea-filled indentations – like Taiohae Bay – and these provide some of the finest anchorages anywhere in the Pacific.

The valleys on Nuku Hiva, which became home to those Polynesian immigrants, are deep and luxuriant. At their heads are waterfalls that spill hundreds of metres from a central plateau, then become streams flowing through forests of miro, mango, mimosa, bamboo, banana, breadfruit and coconut palms. Wild goats, pigs and horses forage among this lush vegetation. In the valleys the Marquesans tended food crops of coconuts, taro, bananas and, most crucially, breadfruit. If the breadfruit crop failed, as it did sometimes through drought, the people starved. The inhabitants emerged only to catch fish from the sea or to wage war on tribes in other valleys. The Marquesans also built great platforms, which they called paepae, out of volcanic stone, and on these the houses of their priests and chiefs were built, carved stone tiki gods were worshipped and human sacrifices made. Another distinctive cultural trait was the elaborate tattoos with which the people adorned parts of, or in the case of some men, their entire bodies.

In 1595 a Spanish voyager, Alvaro de Mendana, came upon the archipelago and renamed the islands the Marquesas, in honour of the Marquise of Mendoza, wife of the Viceroy of Peru. Captain James Cook spent time in their waters in 1774, and in 1791 an American, Captain Ingraham, and later in the same year a Frenchman, Etienne Marchand, visited. In this way the Marquesas were brought to the attention of the outside world.

This marked the beginning of a physical and moral onslaught by Europeans against the indigenous people which, although paralleled in other parts of the Pacific, was exceptional in its brutality. A motley crew of whalers, sailors, traders, ships' deserters and zealous missionaries descended upon the islands, bringing with them a toxic brew of alcohol, avarice, lust, gospels, firearms and infectious diseases. Local men and women were kidnapped and taken to sea on whaling ships. Most never returned. Epidemics of diseases like small-pox carried off thousands more. The population of the group, estimated to be 80,000 in Cook's time, dropped to 20,000 by the 1820s and just 7,000 by the end of the nineteenth century. Even today the population is only 7,500.

The Marquesan holocaust was therefore well under way when Melville and Greene jumped ship. In fact, at the same time the *Acushnet* anchored in Taiohae Bay a French fleet was also there, completing France's annexation of the islands. The chauvinism that accompanied this action drew scorn from Melville, who wrote of it, 'Floating batteries, which lay with their fatal tubes ostentatiously pointed at a handful of bamboo sheds, sheltered in a grove of coconuts!' He understood that what was unfolding on the Marquesas was nothing less than the destruction of an entire culture – the same process that painter Paul Gauguin was to witness and rebel against on another Marquesan island, Hiva Oa, sixty years later. In half a century the Marquesans' traditional culture had been extir-pated by the missionaries, their paepae and carvings looted, often by church and colonial authorities.

It took Melville's ship one and a half years' hard sailing from the United States before it reached Nuku Hiva. Today the island is a three-hour flight from Tahiti. Apart from the Tuamotu archipelago, which appears like coronets of coral against the dark blue ocean, the plane crosses empty sea. The only flat land on Nuku Hiva is in the extreme north-west, so the airport is located there, and after I arrive I have to make the transfer to Taiohae in a hired, four-wheel-drive Chevrolet owned by Pascal, a rangy, nut-brown Frenchman with a blond ponytail.

It's like no land journey I have taken before. There are no sealed roads in the Marquesas, and the trip takes three gruelling hours. Nothing but the gruntiest vehicle could handle these roads, and Pascal's can only just cope. To describe the roads as rough is to be charitable. The experience is like being driven slowly along the bed of a dry, rock-filled stream bed which goes uphill and around precipices and hairpin bends. 'Très raboteux, n'est pas?' mutters Pascal as he wrestles with the steering wheel and the Chevrolet bumps and grinds its way over small boulders. We cross a broad, semi-desert plateau where a few cattle graze, then begin to climb again. After another hour of grinding upwards, near the top of Mt Muake, Pascal stops the vehicle. 'Regardez,' he commands. And, suddenly, I am aware of the literal meaning of the word breathtaking.

The land falls away, sheer on all three sides, forming a huge bowl whose slopes are covered in coconut palms. Taiohae Bay is an enormous caldera, flooded by the ocean on its southern side, sheltered by two enormous rocky headlands and forming that superb harbour. In its grandeur and scale, the bay is utterly majestic. The town and houses lining the curve of its shore appear like multi-coloured embroidery stitched around the hem of a wide green skirt. Pascal shoves his vehicle into gear again, and we begin a long, zigzag descent into Taiohae itself.

Later, in the bar of my hotel by the bay, I meet a tiny Frenchman of about forty. A pixie figure who speaks quaint English, Jean-Marie is obviously a semi-permanent fixture. He tells me he has fled to Nuku Hiva from Hiva Oa, where he was assaulted in a bar by a large Tahitian. Jean-Marie opens his eyes wide and mimes the fracas. 'We quarrel, over a woman,' he says, 'and 'ee 'eets me, twice. *Boom! Boom!*' He ducked the third blow, but still fell unconscious. It was time to change islands.

Jean-Marie prefers Nuku Hiva now, but until the fight had liked Hiva Oa. Particularly, he liked learning about Gauguin, and admired what the artist did in Atuona, taking on the French authorities. He pours himself another beer and says, 'Gauguin, 'ee tells every-wan about the bloody gendarmes and priests and what they do there, stooling the artefacts from z'Marquesans.'

'What about Herman Melville?' I ask. 'Do you know about him?'

''Erman Mel-veel? Of course I know 'eem. 'E wrote the story of Moby's Dick.' He points towards the bay. 'There is a stele to 'eem, just over there.'

'A stele?' I don't know this word.

'Yes.' Seeing my confusion, he throws his hands in the air. 'A plaque, a sign.' He screws up his eyes, searching for the right word. 'A *mon-u-ment.*'

And indeed there is, a large, impressive sculpture and plaque, describing Melville's activities on Nuku Hiva.

Sculpted by a local carver, Kahee Taupotini, the monument was commissioned by the Herman Melville Society in the United States to commemorate the 150th anniversary of Melville's coming ashore at Taiohae Bay on 9 July 1842. The monument seems to have suffered neglect in recent years, and the ironwood trees that line the bay have closed in around it. Still, when I stand on the spot and look up at the ridge high above the bay, I can understand what a feat it was for the two young Americans to have scaled the slope, let alone made it to the Taipi valley.

Even today it is not easy to reach the Taipi. I'm taken there by my host from the hotel, a large Marquesan man called Bruno, in his four-wheel-drive Toyota. These gargantuan four-wheel-drives are the only vehicles that can cope with the Marquesan terrain. Nearly all are Toyotas or Mitsubishis, diesel-fuelled, four-doored, with big-foot tyres. They cost over US$50,000, Bruno tells me as we drag up the mountain. If they're bought on time-payment, the cost rises to about US$75,000. Many Marquesans borrow lots of money to buy one, then can't afford the interest payments, so the bank repossesses the vehicle. Bruno erupts into giggles as he tells me this, indicating that Marquesans share the Polynesian schadenfreude-type sense of humour.

It takes us half an hour just to drive to the top of the amphitheatre of rock that surrounds Taiohae Bay, then another hour of tortuous climbing and winding before the valley appears below us. But it is well worth it. The Taipi valley is a long gouge in the landscape, and its steeply sloping sides are covered with innumerable coconut palms. The crystal-clear river that drains it passes between stands of breadfruit and citrus trees, mangoes and banana palms. The air is scented with wild mint, basil, vanilla and wood-smoke fires; the tidy houses are surrounded by frangipani and hibiscus; the concrete road passing through the village is lined with yellow crotons. Pigs, goats, chickens and roosters roam the valley, while chestnut-coloured horses graze contentedly beneath the trees.

The people are devoutly Catholic, yet the carving of tiki and war clubs is an important source of income, and nearly every adult male is tattooed with traditional motifs. The Marquesan culture proved far more resilient than the nineteenth-century missionaries ever imagined. And the physical remains of the old culture are also very close. The forested hillsides are riddled with relics of the old gods, the paepae and tiki of pre-Christian times. Some modern houses have been built directly on to these ancient paepae, which make rock-solid foundations. Bruno leads me into the forest to see a paepae only a short climb from the road. It's like something out of an *Indiana Jones* movie: huge slabs of mossy rock, gripped and split by the talons of rain-forest trees, awaiting clearance, excavation and restoration.

One by one the ancient paepae are being reclaimed from the forest and their lithic secrets deciphered. One just out of Taiahoe has been completely restored. As we climb up and over the stone platform, Bruno explains that the Marquesans traditionally buried the skulls of their dead in the aerial roots of banyan trees, so that the remains were slowly borne upwards as the tree grew. He points out a banyan tree next to a paepae that recently caught fire. When its core burnt, the ground beneath the tree was showered with skulls.

When *Typee* was published in 1846, Melville was attacked by reviewers who accused him of faking his chronology and setting. For example, in one memorable scene his heroine, the Princess Fayaway, sails a canoe on a large lake, her body making a human mast and her tapa mantle spread wide to catch the wind. Because there is no lake in the Taipi valley, the critics used this to question Melville's general verisimilitude, in the process confusing fiction writing with travel writing and greatly undervaluing the role of the writer's imagination. I am certainly not disappointed when Bruno drives me to the place where the valley opens out and meets the sea. Here a small backwater has been formed by a sand bar blocking the place where the river flows into Controllers Bay. Was this Melville and Fayaway's 'lake'? It may well have been. Even if the subject of a literary conceit, the Taipi estuary is undoubtedly a scene of loveliness: verdant, serene, remote, hemmed in by mountains, forest and sea.

Herman Melville was eventually saved from the critics who labelled him a liar by one Richard Tobias Greene, who wrote a letter to the *Buffalo Commercial Advertiser* testifying to the accuracy of Melville's account. The writer was Toby, Melville's fellow deserter. He had been uplifted from Nuku Hiva before Melville by a French ship and, until learning of Melville's book, had assumed his former companion was dead. A grateful Melville sought out Greene and chronicled his experiences as *The Story of Toby*, which was published as an appendix to the later editions of *Typee*.

Just as the Samoans still claim Robert Louis Stevenson as one of their own, the Marquesans retain an affection for Herman Melville because of his stout defence of their way of life when it was caught in a pincer between ruthless imperialism and missionary bigotry. And the American literati come to Nuku Hiva to see Melville's valley. Bruno tells me that a local guide, using the 'facts' of *Typee* as a reference, even claims to have located the site of the house where 'Marheyo' was held captive. Bruno takes me to the site and points to a paepae just below the road in the upper reaches of the valley. Its close-fitting stones are smothered by trees and vines. 'Will it have a plaque like those writers' houses in Paris?' I ask Bruno, and he laughs. 'And how did the guide prove it was the site of Melville's house?' I persist. 'Did he question the old people?'

'He told me he asked the old people of this valley whose forebears could remember Melville,' Bruno says. Then his face splits into a grin. 'But when I asked them how they knew, they said, "Oh that *must* be Melville's place because the guide told us it was."'

At the head of the valley, past a spectacularly high waterfall that also features in *Typee* and that today generates hydroelectric power, the road climbs tortuously, then crosses a saddle to disclose another breathtaking scene – a panorama of Nuku Hiva's north-east coast and a vast slope of mountainside, entirely covered in coconut palms, which sweeps down to the bay of Hatiheu. The road then snakes down through the forest to the bay and the village on its shore, where there is so little traffic the locals use the main street for petanque. Hatiheu Bay is overlooked by towering volcanic outcrops like cathedral spires, one of which is crowned with a white statue of the Virgin Mary, erected in 1872.

During a long cruise through the Pacific in 1888 in search of a tropical sanctuary to ease his tuberculosis, Robert Louis Stevenson and his family anchored their yacht in this bay. Stevenson extolled the lonely beauty of the place in his writing, lending further literary provenance to Nuku Hiva. Today's Hatiheu's most prominent buildings are a Catholic church, a seafood restaurant and a community hall. Carvers shape tiki and clubs in home workshops, and villagers toss petanque balls on the waterfront street, while the surf surges against the boulder beach only metres away. And deep in the forest behind the village, the paepae of the early Nuku Hivans are being laboriously cleared of their jungle cover.

Driving back from the valley, we pass a young Marquesan man whose upper arms and back are adorned with tattoos. The man's hair is brown, his skin very fair. 'Many white Marquesans, uh?' observes Bruno, who is pale himself. The genes of those nineteenth-century whalers and renegades endure. Later, exploring the village of Taiohae on the edge of the bay, I come across a framed photograph, 'The Last Nuku Hivan Cannibal', hanging on the wall of the mairie, or town hall. It shows an elderly man with a flaring white moustache-less beard who stands staring wide-eyed at the camera, looking more terrified than terrifying, although he bears over his shoulder a hardwood u'u – the great club with which the Marquesans crushed the skulls of their enemies.

On my last night on Nuku Hiva, I'm having a few beers

with Jean-Marie and Bruno when a thin Frenchman of about sixty walks in and orders a bottle of red wine. He has a narrow, flushed face and a markedly receding hairline. He speaks excellent English, and tells me his name is Serge and that he is married to a local woman. We chat about the Marquesas and he tells me how many of the young people – his own children included – have moved away to Papeete, or even France, for their future. The Marquesas Islands, so geographically massive and imposing, are, Serge explains, economically unsustainable. It's only the territorial government in Tahiti, lavishly funded by France, that keeps them going. Virtually everything – transport, education, medicine, power generation – is subsidised.

As I listen to Serge, I notice that he has the worst case of alcoholic trembles I have ever seen. His hand is shaking so much he can hardly get his glass up to his mouth. But he manages, tipping glass after glass down his gullet. In minutes the bottle is empty, he's ordered another and his face has turned the colour of cabernet sauvignon. Then, excusing himself, he says that alas, he has to start work at eleven o'clock tonight. He shakes my hand, bids us all 'au revoir', and slaloms his way to the door. Curious, I ask Bruno, 'What work does Serge do?' The big man gestures with one hand in the direction of the town. 'He works at the hospital. He is the island's surgeon.'

Coming to the Marquesas has in some ways been like arriving at the end of the Earth. I'm due to fly back to Papeete at midday, and Pascal has said that he will pick me up at 8 a.m.

for that punishing, three-hour drive to the airport. But it's a quarter to nine now, I'm waiting by the hotel entrance, and there's no sign of him. Bruno tells me Pascal's gone over to the Taipi valley to pick up some other people first, but when he hasn't shown up by nine o'clock I begin to panic. I have an irrational horror of being stuck here: I *mustn't* miss that flight.

It's now 9.30. Bruno comes out and frowns, sympathetic to my plight. 'Where *is* Pascal?' I ask him.

'You heard the rain last night?'

Indeed I did. It was so heavy it felt as if the whole island were being dumped on by a waterfall.

'Rain has made road very bad,' Bruno says. 'Maybe flooding in Taipi valley. Pascal's truck maybe can't get through.'

Shit! Is there any other way to get to the airport?

Bruno shrugs. 'You could take z'elicopter.'

Really? How much is that? One way, 6,000 francs? I do a calculation, always difficult in French Pacific francs. That's … about … ninety-six dollars New Zealand. I pull out my wallet and count the local currency I have left: six 1,000-franc notes. Exactly the helicopter fare. But if I take the flight, I won't have a single franc left until I get back to Papeete. But then I won't *need* any money once I get to the airport, and I'll get food and drink on the plane. Checking the time, I see that it's already 9.45. Even if Pascal turns up now, we'll probably never make it. My anxiety is verging on panic.

'What time does the next helicopter flight leave for the airport?' I ask Bruno.

'Ten-thirty,' he replies. 'If you like, I'll drive you over to the heliport. It's at the other end of town.'

I have never been in a helicopter before. Now, strapped in beside the French pilot, who bears an uncanny resemblance to Arnold Schwarzenegger, I can hardly hear myself think. The chopper's rotors are noisy and right above our heads. Then Arnold shoves the joystick forward and in an instant we're moving straight upwards. Five seconds later the whole bay of Taiohae is below us. It's a sensation like no other, like being in a bubble – an amazing bubble that does exactly what Arnold wants it to. It is the most giddying, vibrating, yawing, thrilling, terrifying ride of my life. Arnold swoops up the slopes of Mt Muake, across chasms and over cataracts, over the saw-toothed ridges of the sierra; he whips over the desert plateau and down towards the island's north-western corner. On the way he leans forward and grimaces, appearing to battle powerful updrafts which are seizing the chopper and biffing it this way and that. During these moments I'm convinced that the winds will win and we'll plunge to our deaths in the ravine below. But Arnold triumphs and, minutes later, peering down, I glimpse the Virgin Mary statue atop its pinnacle. In another minute the island's runway comes into sight. A few seconds later, and Arnold's lowering us down on to it. It's 10.38. The three-hour transfer by road has taken just eight minutes by helicopter.

The airport terminal is a small modern building with plastic tables and chairs, a bar and a souvenir shop. Ceiling fans churn overhead, but they make little difference to the temperature, which is very hot, nearly forty degrees. The downside of my helicopter ride is twofold: I now have to wait for over two hours for the plane back to Tahiti, and I have absolutely no money left. And I'm getting thirsty. Very thirsty. Very, *very* thirsty. All around me people are drinking from water bottles, fruit-juice cartons and beer cans. Slaking their thirsts, casually, gratefully, pleasurably. I can't even drink from the toilet tap, because the water here is definitely not potable – the island's catchment areas are filled with carcasses of dead pigs, goats and horses.

So I sit, and watch other people drinking, and dehydrate. My mouth is like emery paper, my limbs almost motionless. I feel giddy with thirst – the worst thirst I've ever had. I consider stealing a water bottle from the bar, but it's not possible as they're all in a fridge behind the barman. Instead, I hang my head between my legs and try to salivate. I can't. I'm dying of thirst. I barely register that the terminal door has opened and three people entered, until I see who one of them is. *Pascal*! He made it in his truck after all! I could have come with him, saved myself fifty dollars and still had enough money to buy beer, water, tea, soft drinks – anything to slake this terrible, murderous thirst. Why ever did I take that helicopter?

An hour passes, an hour and a half. I try going outside, but it's like a furnace out there, a shimmering, desiccating, searing heat which in seconds evaporates whatever bodily fluids I have left. Staggering back inside, I take a seat and prepare to pass out. Inside, the heat is still infernal.

Then, through a haze, I see a Marquesan man at the next table put down a large water bottle, then get up and walk away in the direction of the toilet. *The water bottle's two-thirds full.* Staring at it, I know that I have to have it. A French couple are making their way towards the table, and there's no sign of the Marquesan man, so I dash for the bottle, snatch it up and run for the door. Outside, ignoring the scorching heat, I tip up the bottle and let its contents run down my gullet, slowly, thankfully, mercifully. It's the best drink I've ever had – better than the coconut milk on Atiu, better than the finest French champagne, better than the most exotic cocktail. In fact it's not water, it's ambrosia, and it's saved my sanity, if not my life. Conserving the last quarter of the bottle's contents, I put the cap back on and, as I do so, I hear the dronc of an engine. I look across to the west, and see a red and white plane, the Air Tahiti ATR 72. Saved again.

Nuku Hiva, which on the ground was so massive in scale it seemed a place where giants must dwell, is shrunk by height to normal size. There below is Hatiheu Bay and the Taipi valley, then Mt Muake and Taiohae Bay and Bruno's hotel, its thatched bungalow roofs like a cluster of asterisks. Then the mighty island is gone and, after a teasing glimpse of the soaring spire of neighbouring Ua Pu, there are just clouds and the white-capped ocean. Opening my copy of *Typee*, I read the end of its appendix, *The Story of Toby*. After describing the young man departing from Nuku Hiva in the French sailing ship, Melville concludes, 'Toby left this vessel in New Zealand, and after some further adventures, arrived home in less than two years after leaving the Marquesas.'

'Some further adventures'? It's tantalising. Which literary sleuth will put into place the last piece of Toby's puzzle?

NINE

LAUGHTER OF LOUIS
SOCIETY ISLANDS

EVERY EVENING, as the setting sun turns the sky above Tahiti's lagoon the colour of a Provençal rosé, they're out there practising: dozens of six-man canoe teams, brown bodies bent forward, arms rising and falling in unison, slim outrigger canoes scarcely visible above the waterline.

In two days' time it will be the real thing, the start of the annual Hawaiiki Nui Va'a canoe race, three days of paddling across open seas between Huahine, Raiatea, Tahaa and Bora Bora, the Society Islands, half an hour's flight north-west of Tahiti. Canoe racing is an ardent pursuit throughout French Polynesia, as keenly contested as road cycling races are in France.

When, two days later, I arrive at the waterfront town of Fare in Huahine, outrigger canoes are everywhere, having been shipped here on a French naval vessel. The canoes are eight metres long, made in Papeete from moulded fibreglass, brightly coloured and emblazoned with the logos of their sponsors – banks, oil companies, breweries and other French Polynesian firms. Earlier today there was a traditional ceremony to bless the impending race, followed by dancing, feasting and entertainment from a Hawaiian rock band doing excellent covers of the Eagles.

This is the biggest thing that happens in Fare, the capital town of Huahine, an island of towering mountains, secluded villages and deeply indented bays, whose winding roads, lined with breadfruit trees, coconut palms and vanilla plantations, all lead back to the Fare waterfront. On a tour of the island, which is one of the loveliest I've been on, I'm taken to the top of a bluff which overlooks the bay separating Huahine-Nui (Big Huahine) from its neighbour, Huahine-Iti (Little Huahine), the two islands being joined by an elegant bridge. After my guide, a sophisticated French-Tahitian woman called Maria, has pointed out various land features, I ask her, 'What does "Huahine" mean?'

She thinks hard for a moment. '"Hine" is our word for "woman", and "hua" means …' She licks her lips, then concludes with utmost seriousness: 'Hua … you would say in English … is "cunt".' She nods. 'Yes, that's what Huahine means, "Cunt Island".'

Trying not to show my surprise at this information, I reply, 'Oh, well, that must have made it a popular place.' I think again. 'In the old days, I mean.'

Maria nods, thoughtfully. 'Yes.' Then she laughs. 'But it's nice today, too.'

Moored in Fare harbour is my floating home for the next five days, *Haumana*, or 'Spirit of Peace'. She is to follow the marathon canoe race – a kind of Tour de France on water – which has been held every year since 1992. *Haumana* is a thirty-six-metre, three-level catamaran with thirteen cabins, each with full-sized windows, a bathroom and air-conditioning. On the top deck there's a big lounge, bar and open terrace. The cabins are on the middle deck, and the lower deck has a restaurant which seats forty people. An inflatable tender transfers me to the ship, and I immediately rejoice in the air-conditioning. On shore, it's scorching.

'Votre baggage, M'sieur?'

'Ah … oui … merci.'

The crew member, Tomita, picks up my suitcase and carries it to my cabin. The case is heavy but she carries it as if it were a croissant. She wears a tight-fitting red pareo, her black hair is elaborately coiffured and she has a curvaceous figure, including very prominent breasts, but she has the build of a construction worker. Like most of the crew of *Haumana*, she is a raerae, or transvestite. Though initially disconcerting, Tomita and her team become completely accepted by the ship's passengers over the next few days. In the evenings, on the top deck, they dance the seductive Tahitian tamure, put on a fashion parade, weave baskets from pandanus, and play the guitar and ukulele as the sun goes down. They're unfailingly jolly and attentive.

While the canoeists practise on the lagoon, and the music of the Hawaiian band reverberates around the harbour, we have our first evening meal, prepared by a young French chef, Emeric Berthelemy. Befitting a man who has married a Tahitian, his menu is a mélange of French flair and Pacific ingredients: taro soup followed by mahi mahi in a vanilla sauce with green salad, apple and nuts, and a dessert of banana and chocolate pancakes. The taro soup is a little sludgy, but the rest is delectable. Mahi mahi, a prized game fish in the tropical Pacific, is superb eating, and the flavour of its firm white flesh is enhanced by the subtle aroma of the vanilla sauce. Vanilla is the Society Islands' main cash crop, and it thrives in the damp, humus-rich soils.

At 7.30 the next morning a green flag goes up and the canoeists are off. The harbour waters turn to a churning mass as eighty-four outrigger canoes burst away from the start line and head for the passage through the reef. The first destination is Raiatea, whose pastel-grey profile is visible forty-five kilometres due west. It's an island that many New Zealand Maori believe is Hawaiiki, the spiritual homeland of their ancestors. On it stands Taputapuatea, Polynesia's most sacred marae.

Within minutes Huahine's pass has been breached, the field has spread and we're in open sea, pursuing the outriggers. For the purposes of the chase, I've been transferred to a poti marara, or speedboat ('marara' being a flying fish and 'poti' the transliteration of 'boat'). The skipper is a stocky, barefoot Tahitian in his thirties called Louis, who controls his boat from the bow with a vertical PVC rudder. Wearing a baggy yellow singlet, blue shorts and a black back-to-front baseball cap, Louis grins a lot. When he is not grinning he is laughing uproariously and waving to the other speedboat skippers. I've never seen anyone laugh so much. Any boat that passes, anything that anyone calls to him, Louis breaks into hysterical laughter. When we strike a big launch's wake and nearly roll, he laughs so much he almost goes overboard. When one of his mates on another speedboat shouts something at him about his misjudgement, Louis becomes almost paralytic.

But Louis is obviously an experienced operator because he keeps us on course for Raiatea, close enough to the paddling canoeists without interfering with their course, and manages to avoid hitting any of the big pleasure boats which are streaming along beside us. There's a huge flotilla out here now – every type of vessel, from French vermouth palaces whose decks are covered with beautiful topless girls, to wallowing old wooden ferries and an aluminium dinghy containing two Tahitians, a man and a woman, perched on stackable plastic chairs and controlling their little boat with a rope tied to the tiller. Race marshals on jet-skis, stern flags flying, zip around the fleet, keeping it a safe distance from the racers.

And the racing crews are amazing. In thirty degrees of morning heat they're paddling at about sixty strokes per minute, their arms rising and falling in constant unison, kept in regular beat by the calls of the last man of the six, and pausing only to pass water bottles down the line to replace their streaming body fluids. The teams wear sun-hats but no life-jackets, and they dig their paddles ferociously as they propel their canoes over the ocean swells. Even watching from the relative comfort of our boat the heat is enervating. What it must be like in the canoes, sealed in from the waist down and paddling ceaselessly, can only be imagined.

All around us the indigo sea is lumpy, the sky a brilliant blue. Gradually Raiatea comes into sharper focus, its peaks seeming to rise from the sea. The spectator fleet, including our speedboat, streaks ahead to witness the finish on the waterfront at Uturoa, the island's main town. The winning canoe appears, three and a half hours and over 12,000 strokes after starting, to acclaim from the waiting crowd. It's Number 22, sponsored by the oil company which is the leading rival of the race's main sponsor. It's a fine example of ambush marketing, but no one's complaining. Winning has been an heroic achievement.

There's a great welcome for all the crews as they stagger across the line then go ashore for a hose-down at the town marina and a feast. For me it's back to *Haumana* for a few beers to help me recover from the fatigue induced by watching more than 500 superbly fit young men exhaust themselves at sea. I'm also preparing for Emeric's next dinner: poisson cru, shrimps in curry sauce and coconut milk, coconut pie, and fresh pawpaw, mango and melon. In Tahiti the poisson cru is usually bonito, which abounds in the sea outside the reefs. The experts tell me that the secret to preparing the dish is to rinse the cubed fish in sea water, and add the garlic, coconut milk and the juice of fresh limes only about ten minutes before serving it.

There is time the following day for a visit to Raiatea's special locations.

Haumana cruises first into the Baie de Faaroa, a deep ria, or inlet, in the island's eastern coast and a beautiful, sheltered haven. French Polynesia's only navigable river flows down to this bay from an extinct volcano, Toomaru, the island's highest peak. The place where the river debouches into the bay provided an important shipyard for the early Polynesians. Here they converted the giant rain-forest trees into double-hulled canoes, launched them into the bay and set forth on voyages to other, distant parts of Polynesia, including New Zealand. Before a voyage began, the canoe was blessed by priests at their most sacred marae, Taputapuatea, a little way down the coast. *Haumana* ties up to a jetty a stroll away from Taputapuatea. The marae, built right over this level promontory, consists of a large area of weathered coral rock, hundreds of slabs of dark grey stone, hewn flat and laid straight on to the ground to form a huge square. On the lagoonward side, larger slabs of rock have been placed upright in a line, so they resemble a row of high-backed chairs. In front of the row one upright slab stands alone. The dirt between the stones is pocked with the burrows of land crabs.

When we approach a single upright slab of rock, our Tahitian guide pats it affectionately. 'Here victims were sacrificed to the gods Taaroa, Tane or Oro. Since about the eleventh century, many, many human sacrifices have been made here. Their necks were put against this rock and their throats were slashed open with stone knives.'

'Who were these victims?' I ask nervously.

Nodding in appreciation of my interest, he replies, 'The priests chose them. The victims had to be strong and healthy, not people wounded in battle, because the old gods demanded much blood as a sacrifice.'

Wandering across to where the marae meets the sea, I feel both in awe and in fear of this place – awed by its age and size, but uneasy at the thought of so much violent death. At the foot of several of the upright stones are other stones from other places, tributes placed by people who have made a pilgrimage to this vast, sacred site, which is to the Polynesians what Mecca is to Muslims. The guide tells me the stones have come from the farthest extremes of the Polynesian triangle – Hawaii, Easter Island and New Zealand.

The next stage of the canoe race, from Raiatea to Tahaa, is relatively undemanding, being only twenty-six kilometres and confined to the smoother lagoon waters inside the enclosing reefs of both islands. But it's still ferociously contested, with a winning time of just under two hours. At Tahaa's main village, Tapuamu, the crews carry the canoes ashore on their shoulders and wash themselves and their vessels down by the marina, before turning in early. The third, final and longest (fifty-eight kilometre) stage of the race will take place next day between Tahaa and Bora Bora, whose dramatic profile we can already see on the horizon.

Bora Bora is justifiably known as one of the most beautiful islands in the world. Its volcanic core thrusts straight up from the ocean like an ancient green molar. The whole island is enclosed by a lagoon whose waters are varying shades of blinding blue. The coral sands of a ring of motus feather into the lagoon. From the deck of *Haumana*, I'm reminded immediately of the Rogers and Hammerstein musical *South Pacific*. Bora Bora wasn't the model for James A. Michener's mystical Bali Hai – that was an island in Vanuatu – but it could still be the template.

That night I read a short story by Alex du Prel, a European writer who lives on Moorea. The story is about a Polynesian woman on Bora Bora called Madame Dorita. The narrator of the story goes to Madame Dorita's house to fix her washing machine and, while there, sees a beautifully made chest filled with old but perfectly maintained tools. Intrigued, the narrator asks about the chest and Madame Dorita, who is in her fifties, tells him the story of how it came into her possession.

The chest belonged to an American, one of the several thousand soldiers stationed on Bora Bora for nearly four years during World War II. At the age of sixteen Mademoiselle Dorita fell in love with one of the Americans, a young man called Mike, and became pregnant by him. Shortly afterwards the A-bombs were dropped on Hiroshima and Nagasaki, and the Americans pulled out of the bases in Polynesia and occupied Japan. Mike told the girl he had to leave, but promised to return and get her and the baby. He gave her his tool-chest to look after until he did so, showing her how to oil the tools and polish the chest to keep them in perfect condition.

The girl followed his instructions faithfully, even when French soldiers came to Bora Bora to loot the island of everything the Americans had left behind. To stop the chest falling into the hands of the French the young girl carried it into the mountains and hid it in one of the caves where her ancestors placed the bones of their dead. And every week she went there and oiled the tools. Mike never returned. Mademoiselle Dorita bore his daughter, then married a local man and had children by him, but she still believed, thirty-five years after he left, that one day Mike would return to her.

Touched by this tale, the narrator decides to trace the American. During a trip to the United States, he learns at the Department of Veterans' Administration that Mike married in 1951, had a family, and is now living in the small town of Rio Minas, New Mexico. He drives there to meet him.

He finds himself in a small, dusty town, hostile to outsiders and palpably illiberal in outlook. He has no difficulty finding Mike, but does not disclose the real purpose of his visit. Mike Shay is a pillar of the small, inward-looking community, and only too pleased to talk about 'his' war. When the conversation is steered towards Bora Bora, he talks of the island in great detail, but never once mentions Madame Dorita. When at last the narrator raises the issue of fraternisation with local women, the American becomes first secretive, then confiding. Yes, he had had local girls during his time on Bora Bora – 'native women', as he calls them. He even had a 'Jap' girl later on, in Nagoya. Mike, it seems, is an old-fashioned Southern racist who hardly gave his Polynesian lover a second thought.

The narrator concludes his story by saying that he never told anyone about his trip to New Mexico and that, as far as he knows, Madame Dorita continues to shine Mike's tools and keep them in the beautiful chest. The story, called 'The Hope Chest', ends with some interesting statistics. The 4,400 Americans stationed on Bora Bora during World War II fathered 132 children by local women. Only one came back to get his vahine and marry her.

Not long afterwards, while on Moorea, I look up Alex du Prel and discover he publishes *Tahiti Pacifique*, a monthly magazine of political comment and cultural issues of French Polynesia and Pacific islands, a courageous enterprise. A balding, shambling bear of a man, Alex greets me genially and suggests we go out to lunch at a nearby waterfront village.

There, over Hinano beer, we chat and commiserate over our fates, the way writers inevitably do when they meet. Then I ask Alex, because his nationality seems a little obscure, 'Where were you born?' In the US Virgin Islands, he tells me, to an American father and a German mother. When? 'Nineteen forty-four,' he replies. Same year as me. 'Which month?' He puts his beer glass down. 'January. I'm a Capricorn.' I stare at my companion. 'Date?' 'The fifteenth,' he replies, matter of factly. 'That's my birthday, too,' I say. We burst out laughing, then drink a toast to each other. For the first time in my life I have met a twin.

Unusually, there's only one navigable passage through Bora Bora's reef, Teavanui, on the island's western side. Now the whole fleet – outriggers, speedboats and spectator vessels – is streaming towards it. The sea is again swelly, the going very tough for the canoeists. Louis speeds and swerves his boat among the swells, shouting at his mates in the other boats and laughing hysterically at everything they say when they shout back. Flying fish, startled out of the water by the flotilla, skim the water ahead of us.

It's three and a half hours before the canoes sweep through the passage, cross the wide lagoon and dig their way into Matira Bay, where they are greeted with acclaim by locals, visitors, a battery of news photographers and Monsieur Gaston Flosse, French Polynesia's president, who looks just like New Zealand novelist Maurice Gee. Several of the out-rigger crews collapse with heat exhaustion and have to be revived by first-aid workers. Astonishingly, after dropping me off in the shallows by the beach and seeing who's won the race

—Te Pae Ti'a from Rangiroa atoll in the Tuamotu archipelago —
Louis the boatman turns his speedboat around and stands in
the bow, revving the engine.

'What are you doing?' I ask. 'Aren't you coming to watch
the show?'

Louis points at the horizon and shouts, 'No. I go back now.
Home to Huahine. *Fishing tomorrow!*' He gives his insane laugh
once more, pulls his baseball cap down hard on his head, waves
goodbye and guns the motor, heading for Teavanui Pass and
the long open-sea crossing back to Fare. He hasn't even set
foot ashore.

Tahitian dance teams perform on a barge moored just off
Matira beach. Gaston Flosse makes a speech and presents the
trophies. Gaston, born on Mangareva Island in the Gambier
group, has been president of the French Polynesia Territorial
Assembly continuously since 1991 and for other terms before
that. He has, in every sense of the word, done very well for
himself. In 2002 a Paris court cleared him of corruption
charges, and in 2003 his territory was paid an official visit by
his close friend and patron, French president Jacques Chirac.

Gaston's slogan could well have been 'Polynesie Français,
c'est moi'. France gives its most prized overseas territory
many millions of dollars of development money every year.
Gaston, now in his seventies, also has a great fondness for
beautiful young women – his latest wife is in her early twenties. (Later, in May 2004, the unthinkable would happen:
Gaston Flosse was voted out of office and replaced as president
by a long-time pro-independence campaigner, Oscar Temaru.
A new political era for French Polynesia had begun.)

The winning Hawaiiki Nui Vaka teams are interviewed for international television, then it's party time again. The Hawaiian rock band pounds out its Eagles numbers while food and drink are served in a big marquee by the beach. In the evening there's a dance in nearby Anau village. The transvestites from *Haumana* – Tomita, Sabine, Sophie and Tiare – attend, wearing their best frocks and high heels. But it's been a big day, and no one stays late. We stroll back to the wharf under the stars, then transfer by launch to *Haumana*. As we glide across the lagoon in the warm blackness, the guitar strains of 'Hotel California' echo out from the marquee, where the canoe teams are still celebrating their achievement.

Hawaiiki Nui Va'a is one of the great sporting events of the South Pacific, a testimony to discipline, endurance and fortitude. Watching the crews pack up their canoes, then leaving *Haumana*, I'm aware that I've witnessed something very special over these last few days. Before we climb into the boat's tender and motor away to the airport, Tomita beams goodbye, murmurs, 'Au revoir M'sieur Graeme,' and kisses me hard on both cheeks, her dark whiskers rasping my face. When I'm a safe distance away, I blow back a double kiss.

Later, as my plane soars over Bora Bora and heads east for Huahine, I stare down at the lagoon, the motus, the main town of Vaitape and the island's three great mountains, Otemanu, Pahia and Hue. I'm wondering in which mountain Madame Dorita hid her Hope Chest.

TEN

HOW TO HAVE
A HONEYMOON
LEEWARD ISLANDS

I AM SITTING WITH my new Tahitian friend Armand in the middle of Topatii. Topatii must be the smallest of all of the Leeward Islands of French Polynesia. No bigger than a tennis court, no higher than a wine bottle above sea level, and covered with ironwood trees, it lies in the middle of the largest passage in the reef on the eastern coast of Huahine. All around it, deep turbulent water streams through the breach from the Pacific Ocean, driven by a hot strong trade wind.

Armand and I have come out to the tiny motu in his outrigger to snorkel, but the wind is too strong, so we're sitting on the powdery white sand under the ironwood trees, talking. Armand is about twenty-five, solidly built but not fat. He has a mop of thick black hair, a flattened nose, a silver ring through one earlobe and wraparound sunglasses which are usually shoved up on his forehead. Intricate traditional tattooes adorn his wrists. He could be Maori, from Rotorua, or Kaitaia, but he is a Huahinian and a descendant, he assures me, of Omai, the young Raiatean who was taken to England by Cook's 1774 expedition. On the wall of the hotel where I'm staying, and where Armand works, there's a huge mural of Omai, standing proud in traditional costume.

Armand speaks Tahitian, French and English with equal facility. 'Tell me something,' he says, very serious all of a sudden. 'I have heard that in New Zealand you drive on the wrong side of the road. Is that true?'

'We drive on the left, yes.'

Frowning, Armand draws a highway in the coral sand with his hand, a median strip with his finger. 'You drive – ' he makes an arrow on the left – 'on *this* side?'

'Yes.'

'What about the car steering wheel? That is on the left too?'

'No, the steering wheel is on the right.'

'Ay-yay-yay! On the *right*?'

'Right.'

Armand is even more perplexed now. '*Why* do you drive on that side?' he asks.

'I suppose because we were settled by the British, and they drive on the left.'

'So ... you must change gears with your *left* hand?'

'That's right.'

'And the cars have to be specially made like that?'

'Well, yes, but they're mostly made in Japan, and the Japanese drive on the left too.'

'*They* do too?'

'I'm afraid so. And the Australians, and the Indians. But nearly everyone else in the world drives on the same side as you.'

Armand nods, seemingly satisfied. He gets to his feet and brushes the sand from his blue pareo. 'Okay, we go to Faie village now.'

Ten minutes later he guides the big outrigger into the still water of the Faie inlet. This notch in Huahine's eastern side is surrounded by hills, with stands of coconut palms at sea level and, above them, delicately fronded, flat-topped acacia trees. Small clearings on the hillsides are planted with grey, spiky pineapple plants. Amid the luxuriant greenery, they look like sea urchins in a rock pool.

At the head of the inlet Armand ties up to a jetty beside a cluster of other outriggers. As we get out he picks up a bucket from the canoe; in it is the meaty blue-black head of a large tuna.

Faie, three minutes' walk away, consists of one street of houses, a couple of stores and a new Adventist church. Large mango, breadfruit and citrus trees line the little street. Towering above them, ramparts of volcanic rock, hundreds of metres high, enfold the village. They are covered in dark green bush, and are so high that only a sliver of sky is visible.

Today is Sunday but, being Adventists, the people of Faie village carried out their devotions yesterday, so the shops are open. Children are playing marbles in the dusty street and men are playing petanque alongside them. They greet Armand enthusiastically in Tahitian, joke and laugh as he passes. The difference between the French and Tahitian tongues is marked, and most obvious when Tahitians get together. The latter is guttural, clipped and vowel rich, and comments are inevitably followed by a burst of high-pitched laughter. Tahitians seem to find almost everything a joke.

A small stream channelled by low concrete walls cuts right across the village street. Armand gets down into the stream just below a bridge. The water is very clear and shallow, coming to just above his ankles, and the bed is covered with small round stones. The roots of a huge mango tree have grown down from the concrete wall into the water. I stand on the bank and watch Armand hold the tuna head under the water beside the tree roots and waft it gently to and fro in the slow current. A couple of village men sit on top of the concrete wall on the other side of the stream, smoking and staring down at a sight they must have witnessed many times. A few children, most holding cans of Pepsi, stand behind them, giggling.

Within a minute the first head appears, emerging tentatively from the shadows beneath the tree roots. Then another appears, and a third and a fourth, a row of waving heads and watchful eyes. Then they emerge fully, their sinuous bodies waving gently in the current. There are about a dozen of them. Giant eels. They converge on the tuna head, the smaller ones being shoved aside by a couple of massive ones whose bodies, as thick as a man's thigh, twist and turn as they gorge on the pink fish meat.

Eeling was a popular pastime of mine when I was a boy. There was something mysterious – even sinister – about the ebony-hued creatures which dwelt in the dark recesses of rivers and lakes in my neighbourhood. Catching them was like hunting, but we never contemplated eating them: they were too repulsive. These Faie eels are dappled, not black like New Zealand eels, but their eyes are just as scary – the same repellent pale blue. There are so many of them tearing at the hapless tuna head that it resembles Medusa with the serpents. Armand tells me that the eels are sacred to the villagers of Faie, as one of their ancestors is believed to have been an eel himself. They feed their eels the offcuts of the fish they catch in the lagoon, and never harm them.

When Armand gouges out the tuna's eyes and tosses them into the water, the eels go into a frenzy. The largest, a monster a couple of metres long, pushes the rest away, swallows an eyeball, then slides backward into his lair, his watchful head still protruding. I think how easy it would be to spear him.

Armand sees me staring, and laughs. 'You want to hold him? He won't mind.'

He scoops up another one, only a fraction smaller, and strokes its side as if it were a cat. 'Like this, see?'

'Not today, thanks.'

Later we sit under a tree in the village with a shopkeeper and his wife, drinking Pepsi and eating warm butter cake flavoured with locally grown vanilla. The shopkeeper wears only a yellow pareu, and his big belly is brown and perfectly round. Armand tells him something in Tahitian and the other man's eyes grow huge with disbelief. Looking at me incredulously, he exhales and says, 'Aaaaaeeee …'

'What did you say?' I ask Armand.

He swallows some cake. 'I told him that in your country the cars go on the wrong side of the road.'

It is honeymoon season in the South Pacific. Couples come from the United States, Germany, France, Switzerland, Japan and Italy, but mainly from Italy. Tahiti and its surrounding islands are especially popular with young Italians, and they and the other honeymooners make up most of the guests at my hotel in Huahine. The other group are geriatric French couples, so that surrounding me are either the young and the beautiful or the elderly and the decrepit, with only me in the middle.

It's interesting to sit and study the honeymooners. They are like a separate species, something from a David Attenborough documentary, as they carry out their post-courtship rituals. They change outfits several times a day, depending on whether they're strolling beside the lagoon, lounging by the pool, having lunch or having dinner. And although they do a lot of public touching and eye-gazing, you can tell that, for some of them, things are not quite as idyllic as the pre-wedding publicity led them to believe. The new husbands often look distracted, the new wives have an edge of anxiety.

One couple catches everyone's attention because they are so physically striking. He is American, about twenty-four, tall, with dark, fashionably cut short hair, a Roman nose and clear green eyes. He walks about the hotel with the confidence and command of a young courtroom lawyer on the way up. She is tall too, and fair, her long blonde hair tumbling down over her shoulders. Her face is not as beautiful as his, but her figure compensates. She has the long, perfect legs and the erect carriage of the catwalk. From her deportment and constant change of clothes, she can be nothing but a Californian model. Both are bronzed, and neither will need cosmetic surgery for at least five years. I come to think of them as Lance and Carol.

Lance and Carol have what is called an 'overwater bungalow', a unit connected to the rest of the resort by a narrow wooden bridge. Many times a day Carol walks over the bridge, bearing coffee, fruit juice, beer and cocktails on a tray from the bar. The recipient of all these fluids, Lance, emerges from the bungalow mainly for meals, dressed in designer jeans, boat shoes, and a floral shirt open to the navel to reveal his hairless chest and glittering gold chain. Carol hangs on his arm, and as they pass the bar and the mural of Omai on their way to the dining room, for the benefit of the other guests – and in particular the elderly ones – she nuzzles Lance's neck and slides her long fingers over his tight buttocks.

I thought I was the only one to notice these performances until I met Mario and Gina, from Italy, who joined me on a trip around Huahine in Armand's outrigger. They are honeymooners too. Mario is small and athletic; Gina is tall and powerfully built. He is a telecommunications technician and a soccer player; she is a physiotherapist and a top softballer. Gina, Amazonian in her bikini, swims a lot; Mario, swift and nimble, plays football on the beach with the Tahitian guys who work at the hotel. They all want Mario, whom they call Ronaldo, on their side.

The difference between Lance and Carol and Mario and Gina is marked. The Italians are perfectly natural – they don't act out honeymoon roles. But you can tell they are a well-matched pair who enjoy each other's company. I suspect they've probably lived together for some time.

Mario, Gina and I are sitting at the bar talking rugby – the presence of John Kirwan as coach of the Italian side, Kirwan's Italian family and his team's modest performance at the World Cup have popularised rugby in sports-crazed Italy – when Gina nudges Mario: 'Look, therra she goes again ...'

It is Carol, striding through the hotel lounge bearing a tray holding two garish cocktails with straws sticking out of the tall glasses. Other heads turn at the sight of her long, slim legs, tiny shorts and golden hair. The eyes of three elderly Frenchmen sitting by the bar grow bulbous as they track her movements. Carol walks majestically across the bridge, then disappears into the bungalow.

Gina laughs. 'I theenk she does thees all day, working for heem.'

'It's what they call room service,' I suggest. 'Usually it's the hotel staff who provide it, though.'

'I wonder,' muses Mario, 'for how long she will do thees.'

'Never once have I seen heem take her anytheeng,' adds Gina. 'I think he ees very ... uh ...' She gropes for the right word.

'Spoilt?'

'Si, spoilt. He is very spoilt.'

They go off to see the eels being fed and I go off to borrow a bike to ride around the island to Fare. Cycling is my favourite way to enjoy a tropical island. You go fast enough to cover the ground but slow enough to absorb the sights and scents. I pedal through Maeva village, past the store, church, volleyball court and newish museum – Huahine's lagoon, Lac Fauna Nui, is an enormously important archaeological site – and along the narrow plain that lies at the foot of the pyramid-shaped mountain, Maua Tapu.

The plain is a tangle of banana and coconut palms, bougain-villea, frangipani, breadfruit trees and a smothering creeper called pohue. Every few hundred metres there is a house set among the foliage, with an outrigger tied up on the shore of the lagoon. Interspersed with the rampant vegetation there are small plots of vanilla plants; roadside stalls sell packets of the fragrant orchid pod, along with mangoes, pineapples and bananas. It's hot and there is a soft head wind, but the going is flat and easy. In forty minutes I'm in Fare.

Both Captain Cook and Bligh of the *Bounty* knew Fare's sheltered bay well. It afforded them deep anchorage, and its level, fertile hinterland provided much-needed food crops. But Cook's relationship with Fare and Huahine was much more personal than Bligh's. It seems that Cook came to regard Omai almost as a foster son. Returning from England with him in 1777, Cook left him here, in a substantial house filled with provisions, including arms and ammunition. Omai's worldliness and European possessions, especially his firearms, made him a popular figure. He died of a fever several years after Cook's departure.

Today Fare is an attractive waterfront town with many trees in its main street and a long line of two-storey shops, cafes and pensions. There is a supermarket and a yacht club beside the marina, and children dive from the concrete wharf into the harbour's deep, beautifully clear water. I park my bike against a tree and watch the activities. Trucks filled with plantation produce are backed up on the wharf and crowds of people of all ages are sitting about, leaning against their vehicles. Staring out to sea, I recognise the reason for the bustle and crowds. Out in the bay, heading for the passage, is a small orange cargo ship.

The *Taporo IV* plies the waters between Tahiti, Raiatea, Bora Bora and Huahine, carrying cargo and deck passengers. I watch her swing with surprising speed against the wharf. Everything turns to organised chaos: mooring lines are tossed ashore and, even before they're made secure, a gangway is down, passengers are descending and cranes are swinging into action. A cargo door crashes open, a ramp is hastily lowered, and a new model Renault drives down it and speeds away. A container is connected to cables and hauled on deck; jandal-wearing Tahitian passengers clutching bags and rolled-up sleeping mats climb aboard; and in only about twenty minutes *Taporo IV* is on her way again, bound for neighbouring Raiatea.

Before the airlines came and runways were built beside the lagoons, all South Pacific travel must have been like this. Almost every year another island gets a much-needed runway and regular air connection with Tahiti. As I pick up my bike and ride away from the wharf, I can't help feeling some regret that the days of scheduled inter-island passenger transport by sea are passing into history. It's hard to get romantic over a squat inter-island plane called an ATR 42. Islands are meant to be approached by sea.

My short flight to Raiatea leaves early next morning.

Before dawn I sit in the hotel lobby waiting for my transfer to Huahine's airport. There was a young, heavily pregnant Tahitian woman behind the desk in the lobby when I arrived, but she went outside a couple of minutes ago and now I'm sitting alone in the semi-darkness, staring at the high, woven pandanus ceiling, the shell chandelier and another mural of Omai.

Suddenly a man bursts in through the entrance and looks about wildly. It is Lance. He is chainless, shoeless and wearing only red shorts. He is unshaven and his hair is unbrushed. Seeing me, he demands, 'You speak English?'

'Yes.'

'Is there anyone official here?'

'There was a woman here a minute ago, but she went outside.'

At that moment, the woman reappears in the hotel entrance. Lance turns to her and asks urgently, '*Have you got any medicine?*'

She points to a closed door. 'Medicine in there. But it is locked. Not open till seven.'

Lance simulates strangulation, clicks his tongue, stares about apoplectically, swallows to try and gain self-control. Then, inhaling deeply, he fixes the woman with his gaze and says, slowly but still breathlessly, 'I need toilet paper, lots and lots of toilet paper. And I need water. Lots and lots of fresh water. *Toilet paper and water*, you understand?'

The woman frowns, nods nervously. 'In the toilet, there is paper.' She points across the lobby to another door. 'In there. I will get you water from the kitchen.'

Lance nods. His tanned, usually handsome face is ashen, his hands are trembling. He sprints over to the toilet to gather up paper. The woman slips off in the direction of the hotel kitchen. Outside, in the growing light, the airport van draws up. I pick up my suitcase. Time to go.

ELEVEN

THE GRAVE OF GAUGUIN
TAHITI & THE MARQUESAS

T HE NEWS WHIRLED through the Marquesan village of Atuona like a cyclone. *Le peintre est mort*: the painter is dead. The French artist, recently sentenced to imprisonment for libelling a local gendarme, had died in bed at his house, Maison du Jouir. Everyone knew how ill the fifty-five-year-old had been: half-blind, suffering from tertiary syphilis, his legs covered with suppurating ulcers, his mind addled with alcohol and the pain-killing drugs he injected himself with. But the news of his death from heart failure still shocked the villagers. And what now, his friends wondered, would become of the artist's house, his paintings, books, erotic carvings and pornographic photographs?

The date was 8 May 1903, and the painter, Paul Gauguin, would come to be recognised as one of the greatest artists the world has known.

By dawn the following morning, in the steaming heat of Atuona, Gauguin's body was already in an advanced state of decomposition. With what must have been considerable relish, the Catholic bishop, who had been an implacable enemy of Gauguin's, decided that the artist would be buried immediately at Calvary, the town's Catholic cemetery. The interment proceeded. Months later, Gauguin's goods were auctioned in Atuona. Among the bidders were the Catholic authorities and the town's gendarmerie.

Paul Gauguin had arrived in Atuona, on the island of Hiva Oa, in 1901, but his turbulent life in the South Pacific had begun a decade before. Rebellion and a love of exotica were in his blood. The child of a radically minded Parisian journalist father and a Peruvian Creole mother, the infant Gauguin was taken with his family to Peru after the unsuccessful 1848 Paris revolution. His father died before they arrived, leaving Aline, Gauguin's mother, to raise her two children in Lima. After six years they returned to France, because of the family's straitened financial circumstances. At the age of seventeen Gauguin went to sea as a merchant mariner, travelling the world for several years, stimulating his eclectic taste in art. Andean ceramics, Japanese prints, Javanese carvings, Egyptian frescos – his growing fascination with these exotic arts prefigured the characteristics that his own art would develop.

At the age of twenty-five Gauguin married Mette Gad, a Danish woman. He worked successfully as a stockbroker, the couple had five children and the family lived comfortably for ten years. But gradually the impulse to create his own works of art grew stronger. Largely self-taught, Gauguin was at first influenced by the French Impressionists, especially Camille Pissarro. Increasingly restless, yearning for the simple life,

Gauguin found it first among the Breton people. 'I like Brittany,' he wrote in 1888. 'It is savage and primitive.' He produced landscapes and ceramics, but the critics were unimpressed. One dismissed his work as 'Synthetist'.

By the late 1880s, Impressionism's preoccupation with visual effects no longer satisfied Gauguin. Now he was driven to depict interior states rather than surface appearances. A visit to Panama and Martinique in 1887 furthered his enthusiasm for the tropics. The brightness of the sky, the darkness of the people, the lush colours of the flora captivated him. From now on only the truly exotic would liberate his artistic spirit. What he desired was remoteness, a life among a people whose primitive art had its origins in antiquity – and to do so it was necessary for him to turn his back on his family and France and seek artistic fulfilment somewhere far from European civilisation. It was a dream that many artists have had, before and since, but one that was to assume its most extravagant manifestation in the life and death of Paul Gauguin.

As for a destination, there was no shortage of choice. In 1890 French imperialism was at its height, in West Africa, Madagascar, Indo-China and the South Pacific. The Society Islands, including Tahiti, had been ceded to France in 1880. Influenced by a book he had recently read, Gauguin rejected his initial choice, Madagascar, in favour of the fabled, beautiful island of Tahiti. The book was *The Marriage of Loti*, by popular French author Pierre Loti. Loti's idealised story was based on his relationship with a fourteen-year-old Tahitian girl. Both theme and setting appealed to Gauguin.

Tahiti's laissez-faire morality evidently offered sexual as well as artistic possibilities for a man for whom the exotic and the erotic seemed synonymous. It is likely too that Gauguin was influenced in his choice of destination by photographs of Tahiti by Charles Spitz, who had visited the island in the 1880s and exhibited his work in Paris. At least two of Gauguin's Tahitian paintings – 'Pape Moe' (Mysterious Water) and 'Mere et Fille' (Mother and Daughter) – derive unmistakably from Spitz photo-graphs, but the paintings exude a much greater power. Poor Spitz. With a few brushstrokes, Gauguin eclipsed the photographer's art.

In 1891 Gauguin set sail for Tahiti, arriving in Papeete harbour on 8 June.

Almost immediately, things threatened to fall apart. With his hair worn shoulder-length, like a French Buffalo Bill, and sporting a cowboy-style hat, Gauguin found himself the object of derision. The Tahitians taunted him with cries of 'taata vahine' – man-woman – and his compatriots were no better. Colonial Papeete was highly Frenchified, snobbish and racist. Gauguin had come right around the world only to find another version of what he had run from.

He quickly fell out with the authorities. He openly took a young Tahitian mistress, and constantly criticised French rule. Also, he found that there was almost no indigenous art in Tahiti. Instead, the people expressed their cultural beliefs in song, dance, ceremony and sex, sometimes simultaneously. There *was* the type of art he admired in French Polynesia – marvellous carvings in wood and stone – but, as he was to learn, this lay in the Marquesas Islands, 1,400 kilometres away.

To escape the constraints of Papeete, Gauguin moved to the far side of Tahiti, where he hoped he would become closer to the indigenous people. He did so, literally. While exploring the Faaone district he met a local family and, as part of Tahitian hospitality, was offered their thirteen-year-old daughter, Tehamana, for a common-law wife. He accepted the offer gratefully, and the couple settled at Mataiea, on Tahiti's south coast.

Tehamana subsequently became the subject of many of Gauguin's paintings, an Eve-like figure whom he portrayed both clothed, in mission dress, and naked. At last Gauguin was realising his ambition. In flesh and spirit, he was now at one with the Tahitians, his *fin de siècle* yearning for the simple, natural life partly fulfilled, and he was creating paintings which embodied his beliefs. The paintings from this first Tahitian period are mostly of heavy-limbed, brooding Polynesian women, in settings incorporating mythological Eastern symbols. What strikes the eye is the vibrancy of the colours, the depth of melancholia in his subjects' expressions, the languor of their poses and the presence of his enigmatic symbolism. For example, in 'Arearea no Varua Ino' (Words of the Devil, 1894), a large, dog-like creature skulks in the foreground before two seated, pensive Tahitian women. Does this canine creature symbolise the evil spirit? And if so, why? In the same painting, three small female figures in the background appear to be worshipping a stone god, striking poses similar to those in ancient Javanese temple carvings. And in the painting 'Mana'o Tupapa'u' (The Spirit of the Dead Watching, 1892), a naked, prone young Tahitian woman is being observed on her bed by a sinister, hooded crone, probably symbolising a Polynesian death spirit. 'One of those legendary demons and spectres,' wrote Gauguin, 'the tupapa'us that filled the sleepless nights of her people.' The young woman is Tehamana, but what do the strange bursts of brilliant light in the background represent?

In spite of his artistic output, Gauguin was unable to make ends meet, and in 1893 he decided to return to France to exhibit his Tahitian paintings. He expected they would fetch high prices, establish his artistic reputation and solve his financial problems. The return was disastrous. Of the forty-four paintings shown in Paris, only eleven sold, and there was cutting criticism of his work. Even his former mentor, Pissarro, was unimpressed. Of Gauguin's paintings, he wrote, 'He is always poaching on someone's ground; now he is pillaging the savages of Oceania.' There were other problems too. Gauguin's marriage was in tatters. He took up with Annah, a Javanese girl he picked up on the streets of Paris, and took her to Concarneau. There he got into a fight over her and his ankle was broken. The break never healed properly and caused him great pain for the rest of his life.

Rejected by the Paris art world, his personal life in chaos, there was only one place Gauguin could seek refuge. A small inheritance from an uncle and the sale of a few of his paintings provided him with some funds, and in July 1895 he sailed again for Tahiti. On the way he had an enforced ten-day stopover in Auckland because the ship he was to catch to Papeete had broken down. He stayed in the Albert Hotel in Queen Street, and visited the city's Art Gallery and Museum, where for the first time he saw true Polynesian carving – work of the New Zealand Maori. Art historians see this exposure as having an influence on Gauguin's later work, which includes traces of the Maori art he had observed.

Gauguin's second period in French Polynesia was marked by extreme physical and mental hardship. With his health deteriorating, and devastated by the news of the death of his only daughter, Aline, from pneumonia in 1898, he tried to kill himself by going into the mountains (where his corpse would be eaten by ants) and taking arsenic. The poison induced severe vomiting, and this saved his life.

But the paintings were still coming, and he now had a dealer in Paris, Ambroise Vollard, to advance him money for his work. He was painting on coarse copra sacking, which gave added texture, and this second period in Tahiti saw the creation of his 1897–98 masterpiece, 'D'où Venons-Nous, Que Sommes-Nous, Où Allons-Nous?' (Where Do We Come From? What Are We? Where Are We Going?). The painting is an allegory, blending Polynesian female figures with Oriental symbols in a magical landscape. Gauguin himself wrote of it: 'I have finished a philosophical work on a theme comparable to that of the gospel.' Today beyond price, the painting hangs in the Museum of Fine Arts in Boston.

Personally, however, Gauguin had reached the depths of despair on Tahiti, and his long-held yearning to escape to the Marquesas had become irresistible. In a letter to a friend in July 1901, he wrote: The 'savage surroundings ... will revive in me, before I die, a last spark of enthusiasm which will kindle my imagination and form the culminating point of my talent.' Leaving his pregnant vahine, Pau'ura, behind in Punaauia, he set sail for Atuona, on the Marquesan island of Hiva Oa, arriving there on 16 September 1901.

There is no place on Earth quite like the Marquesas Islands. Remote and wild, with mountains, plateaus, ravines and cataracts of dark grandeur and breathtaking beauty, the Marquesan landscape is so massive that it shrinks the human presence to Lilliputian size. Waves smash against cliffs and headlands, and torrential rains swell the rivers which pour down from the mountains, turning the sea the colour of onion soup.

Atuona lies at the head of the Bay of Traitors, overlooked by a towering mountain, Temetiu, which rises abruptly from the coast. A sultry, sweltering place, Atuona is dank with humidity and the rich smell of tropical vegetation. Here Gauguin bought a block of land from the Catholic bishop and arranged for a house to be built on it. However, he quickly realised that Atuona provided no real escape from civilisation. If anything, colonial conflicts were concentrated even more fiercely in this isolated enclave of French rule, where the gendarmerie was corrupt and the Catholic authorities repressed the indigenous people. Hypocrisy was rife, with the local priest openly having an affair with two sisters.

Inevitably, Gauguin incurred the wrath of the authorities. He took a local girl as a lover, and provocatively named the house he built Maison du Jouir – the House of (Sexual) Pleasure. In it he placed one of his wooden sculptures, Father Lechery, which depicted the local priest as a giant phallus. He produced a subversive broadsheet, entitled *Le Sourire* (The

Smile), and illustrated it with his engravings. He also encouraged the Marquesans to withdraw their children from
French-run boarding-schools and to refuse to pay taxes.

Meanwhile, his artistic energy remained undiminished.
The best-known work of this last period is his haunting
'Riders on the Beach' (1902), a depiction of Marquesans on
horseback at the beach at Atuona, a place which provided a
forum for the airing of grievances, away from the prying eyes
and ears of the town's French authorities. Not long after this
painting was finished, Gauguin's final physical decline began,
culminating in his wretched death.

Today in Atuona there is a bank, a post office, an Air
Tahiti office, a few pensions, snack bars and Chinese-run
stores. In the sticky heat, the Tricoleur hangs limply above the
gendarmerie. There is still a Catholic mission and a boarding-
school.

The day after I arrive, I climb a path at the eastern end of
the town that leads to Calvary cemetery. Here, under a
frangipani tree, lies Paul Gauguin's grave, made of pitted red
volcanic rock and scattered with soft white blossoms. A
fellow tenant of the graveyard is Belgian singer-songwriter
Jacques Brel, who also went to Hiva Oa to seek inspiration
and died there in 1978.

A granite plaque has recently been installed on the
Gauguin grave to mark the centenary of the painter's death.
At the same time Atuona held a three-day celebration of his
life and works. A graveside ceremony was led by two of his
grandchildren, Marcel Tai Gauguin of Tahiti, who designed
the plaque for the grave, and Maria Gauguin of Denmark, the

daughter of one of the painter's sons from his European family. The ceremony was followed by the opening of the Paul Gauguin Cultural Centre, built on the land bought by the artist in 1901. The centre includes an artist's residency and studio, and a reconstruction of Maison du Jouir, whose upper floor is to be be used as an exhibition room to display works by local and visiting artists. Next door is the excavated well which Gauguin used, at the bottom of which important artefacts, including many hypodermic needles from his self-medication, were found.

One morning in Atuona I witness a contemporary example of what must have incensed Gauguin. A line of blue-uniformed teenage girls from the town's Catholic boarding-school is returning from an outing. Open-faced and beautiful, they chatter happily as they amble down the main street. But at the main intersection of the town stands a stooped, elderly nun, whey-faced and wimpled. Reproaching them loudly in French, she shrieks at them to hurry. *Plus ça change, plus c'est la même chose.*

In Tahiti I drive to a well-kept house up a side street in Faa'a, a suburb of Papeete. A slim man with coal-black hair greets me. This is Marcel Tai Gauguin, one of ten children fathered by Emile Gauguin, the son of Paul Gauguin by Pau'ura, the woman who is depicted in one of his most moving paintings, 'Te Tamari No Atua' (Nativity).

Marcel takes me into a large room alongside his house. There, on all four walls, are scores of 'Gauguin' paintings from his Breton through to his Marquesan period – all produced by an Italian, Claude Farina, and his Czech wife, Vierka, who have devoted their lives to copying Gauguins. (Tahitian art experts are divided on the worth of the Farina reproductions. One told me vehemently how much he despised them; another said they're useful simply because they demonstrate that only a true genius could have created the originals.) Marcel stands beside a painting of a recumbent Tahitian woman with a Christ-like child by her bed. 'Te Tamari No Atua'.

I point at the woman. 'Votre grand-mère? La femme de Gauguin?'

Marcel nods proudly, showing no bitterness towards the painter who had abandoned her. 'Oui, Pau'ura. Ma grand-mère.'

Marcel then tells me the story of his father, Emile, who was born after Gauguin left for Atuona. An American woman, convinced that artistic genius must be hereditary, took Emile to Chicago and paid for him to go to art school there. When, after three years, he had produced nothing out of the ordinary, he returned to Tahiti, where he became a well-known figure on the Papeete waterfront, weaving beautiful fish-traps out of bamboo. Emile had many children by his Raiatean wife, among them Marcel, and lived to be over eighty.

Marcel also tells me that he recently had a vision on the beach at Mataiea, where Gauguin lived. It was of something that would come to pass some time after the centenary of his grandfather's death. Marcel will not divulge the details, but he says that he is now the same age as his grandfather was when he died.

'Did the vision suggest that you would begin to paint after the centenary had passed?' I ask.

Marcel only smiles enigmatically. He also tells me that when, in 1901, Paul Gauguin was living with Pau'ura in Punaauia, on Tahiti, and suffering great pain from his various afflictions, he was told by a local shaman that the cause of the physical agony was his depiction of traditional Tahitian images in wood. A European should not have done this, the shaman concluded, and the gods were exacting their revenge. Desperate by now, the artist collected up all his carvings, took them down to the shore at Punaauia and threw them into the lagoon. In this way many of Gauguin's most accomplished works – he was a brilliant carver – were lost forever.

Paul Gauguin may have been dead for a century, his paintings dispersed to galleries in Paris, Moscow, Boston and Chicago, but he is far from forgotten in French Polynesia. Tahitians regard him with affection. 'He was a good guy, he fought for us,' one tells me. He has many descendants living in Papeete and Atuona. At Papeari, alongside one of the loveliest stretches of coastline on Tahiti, is the Gauguin Museum, with exhibits chronicling the artist's life and work, and in Papeete there is the Lycée Paul Gauguin, Tahiti's oldest secondary school. Reproductions of Gauguin's images are everywhere, on souvenir place-mats, trays and chocolate-box lids, while the 360-passenger luxury cruise ship MV *Paul Gauguin* plies the waters of the Society Islands and makes an annual voyage to Hiva Oa in the Marquesas. The painter's Polynesian images can also be seen in Papeete every day, especially in the broad faces of the Tahitian women who tend their produce stalls in the market.

In recent years Gauguin the man has suffered at the hands

of ideologically driven critics. It has become *de rigueur* to condemn his life in Polynesia. These detractors claim that the artist was a colonist, a cultural tourist, a drunkard, a mysogynist and a paedophile. Such retrospective judgements seem pointless. Gauguin certainly behaved badly, but the entire colonial history of the South Pacific is of European men behaving badly. And in this case, had it been otherwise, the world would have been denied Paul Gauguin's marvellous art.

And the Tahitians have forgiven him. In another commemoration of the centenary of his death, the Museum of Tahiti and Her Islands, a few kilometres west of Papeete, exhibited the largest collection of Gauguin originals ever shown in French Polynesia, on loan from Paris's Musée D'Orsay. *Ia Orana Gauguin* featured five major paintings and the famous ceramic sculpture 'Oviri' (Wild), along with engravings, watercolours and drawings. These works – flown out from Paris on four separate flights – were insured at a cost of US$300 million, and a special secure wing built at the museum to accommodate them. There were more visitors to the museum in that two-month period than there usually are in an entire year.

As for Gauguin's revolutionary use of colour, it remains a truism that beauty is in the eye of the beholder. A French-Tahitian friend told me the story of her grandmother, who lives in Papeete. Cleaning out her storeroom recently, the grandmother made a bonfire of the rubbish she had accumulated there and burnt it enthusiastically in the backyard. Seeing the big pile of ashes, my friend asked her, 'What have you been burning?'

'Oh, sacks, papers, old clothes. A few old paintings.'

'Paintings? What were the paintings?'

'Of animals mostly. Dogs, horses. I think my father was given them. Many years ago.'

'Who painted them, Mama?'

'There was a name on them.' The old lady screwed up her eyes. 'The name was ... Gauguin. Somebody Gauguin.'

'*You burnt some Gauguin paintings?*'

The old lady was unmoved. 'Yes. They were foolish paintings.' She shrugged. 'Is a horse blue? Is a dog orange?'

TWELVE

FRENCH LESSONS
TAHITI ITI

TAHITI, OFTEN ASSUMED to be one island, is in fact two. Only an hour's drive, but an entire world away from the sophisticated resort hotels and boutiques of Papeete, is Tahiti Nui's smaller Siamese twin, Tahiti Iti. The two are joined at the waist by a causeway, over which the town of Taravao has been built. Tahiti Iti – Little Tahiti – is relatively undiscovered. It has no resorts, its inhabitants are mainly Tahitian rather than French or mixed race, and there is no road which completely encircles the island.

Some years ago I drove around Tahiti Iti as far as Teahupoo on the southern coast. There the road stopped and a track began. Ever since, I had been nagged by an urge to follow that track, to see if it was possible to hike around the roadless coast. Yes, it was possible, I was informed, but it was tough going and a guide was essential. Inquiries were made, arrangements followed.

'M'sieur Graeme?'

'Oui?'

'Je m'appelle Zena. Je suis votre guide.'

The man's appearance startles me. We are on the deck of the Fare Nana'o, a wonderfully eccentric hotel near the Taravao causeway and the starting point for Tahiti Iti hikes. But my guide is not Tahitian, nor French, nor a mixture of both. He's African, small and slender, with perfectly even, very white teeth and a beard like a bird's nest.

Zena Angelien is an orphan of empire. Born in Madagascar fifty-five years ago, he was drafted into the French army in his teens and sent to Tahiti in the service of the mother country. After seventeen years as a gym instructor at a big army base at Taravao, he left the military, settled on Tahiti Iti and became an expert on the wild side of his adopted island. Zena is accompanied by his dog, a large, ginger, shaggy mongrel called Marcel. Not a dog lover, I eye Marcel warily, but after a couple of sniffs I'm accepted.

Half an hour later, a utility truck calls at Fare Nana'o and collects me, Zena, the dog and the third member of our party, a sixtyish Frenchman called Emile. We're driven along Tahiti Iti's southern coast, through sleepy villages and plantations, and past beaches where Tahitian children frolic in the shallows and French women baste their breasts in the tropical sun. The coastal plain is narrow, crowded with palms, mango and breadfruit trees, and backed by towering mountains. Far out to the right, across the wide lagoon, surfers flash in and out of the reef waves – Tahiti Iti's reef break at Teahupoo is French Polynesia's most famous, and one of the locations for the annual world series surfing competition. Its great waves and tubes – on some occasions bigger even than those off Oahu, in Hawaii – have challenged some of the best board-riders in the world.

Near where the road becomes a track there is a little harbour with an outrigger canoe moored beside a pebbly beach. As we load our packs into the pirogue, I pick up Zena's. Or try to. It's army issue, about a metre high, crammed full, and so heavy I can barely move it. It must weigh about forty kilos. Zena sees me struggling, smiles, comes over and hefts the pack into the boat as if it's a bag of baguettes. Marcel leaps into the bow, then we're off.

The outboard-powered outrigger canoe skims over the silky lagoon water, giving us fine views of Tahiti Iti's mountainous interior. The scale of the broken, bush-clad monoliths is astonishing. Sheer-sided, split into massive ravines, they taper skyward to needle peaks, and are covered in fine mist.

The pirogue rounds a promontory and we pull in alongside a small concrete jetty. The Tahitian boatman lets us off with our gear, then motors off: 'Au revoir, messieurs. Sunday, three o'clock!' It's now midday Friday.

For the French – even French hikers – eating is a sacred activity. The first thing Emile and Zena do is have lunch: bread, cheese, tinned meat, bananas, and red wine from a five-litre cardboard cask. I've sworn off wine during the day, but my two companions have lots, swigging it down from plastic cups. And as Emile drinks, he becomes voluble and intermittently breaks into song.

The Frenchman has a head which seems several sizes too large for his body, a deeply creased face, curly greying hair and a matching moustache, a spigot nose and prominent ears. But although his face is sixty-two, his body is twenty-five – lean, muscular, sinewy and tanned. He attributes this to swimming, kayaking and a vigorous love life. Married and divorced three times, he speaks good English, but frowns when he hears my French.

'We will teach you to speak *good French*,' he growls, making it sound like a threat. Zena smiles benignly and nods. He speaks no English, and his French is so soft and rapid that it's hard for me to understand. But his actions are eloquent. Superbly organised – presumably as a consequence of his army training – he is also imperturbable, and immensely strong for one so slender. In his pack he carries food, drink and cooking equipment for three men for three days. By contrast, I am woefully under-prepared. I have boots, but only one small pack, no cooking equipment and no wet-weather gear except a plastic jacket and an umbrella. I put in a sleeping bag only as an afterthought. My umbrella provokes extreme derision from Emile: 'Regardez, Zena. Il a un parapluie!' Well, why not? I ask him. 'It rains a lot in the tropics, n'est pas?' Already he's getting on my nerves, this overly energetic Frenchman, and I'm tempted to shove my parapluie down his throat. Instead, I pick up my primary school-size pack and the umbrella, and indicate that I'm ready to go.

The walk begins, with Emile leading, me in the middle, Zena at the rear and Marcel roaming all over the place. The track follows the coast closely, at first through groves of coconut palms and breadfruit trees, then, after the plain tapers away, around steep hills covered in vines and the tangled roots of rain-forest trees. The weather is fine now, but recent heavy rain has left the ground sodden and muddy underfoot. We make our way slowly along the puggy track, with the sea still visible below to our right. Emile loves singing English nursery rhymes, and the strains of 'Three Blind Mice' – an insensitive choice in the circumstances – ring through the forest. La boue – the mud – and the steeply sloping, rocky ground make the going heavy and slow.

Emile has his first fall about half an hour after lunch. In view of the amount of wine he's had, it's unsurprising. He goes over in slow motion, the weight of his pack tipping him sideways before he lands heavily on a rock. I go to assist but he's already on his feet again, waving me away. Only his Gallic pride seems wounded. (He slips and falls many times over the next three days, and I quite like it when he does, not least because it stops him singing nursery rhymes for a while.)

As the track rises across an escarpment, the forest becomes denser. The roots of the huge trees present both an obstacle and a hand-hold. Their fallen leaves – yellow and wet like outsized, soggy cornflakes – sometimes act as matting and sometimes slide away treacherously under our feet. Glossy skinks dart from the track at our approach, but there is no sign of bird life.

Crossing the many streams that tumble down from the mountains makes different demands. The black rocks are round, mossy and terribly slippery, while the stream banks rise so steeply that the going is strictly hand over hand. Slip-sliding away, we cross the streams, scale their banks and make our way slowly up and through the forest. Through the trees to our right, far below, is the sea, pale blue and translucent, its floor embroidered with pink coral formations.

Three hours, one more stream and slope later, the ground levels out. 'Our camp,' declares Emile. It's an area of bare brown earth, littered with leaves, interlaced with thick tree roots and overhung with the canopy of enormous buttressed trees. Zena unpacks and erects our 'tent', a blue plastic tarpaulin slung over a rope between two trees, but there is no groundsheet. From this primitive encampment it's a quick, muddy slide down a steep bank to a coral sand cove, backed by lava cliffs and fronted by rock pools and the reef.

Club Med it isn't, but as the sun begins to sink in the sky Zena dismembers a supermarket duck with a small cleaver, and over an open fire in the clearing cooks a deliciously spicy meal of what he calls 'canard Madagascar', which the three of us eat by firelight, with red wine. We toss the bones to Marcel, who crunches them up and swallows them effort-lessly. Emile is turning out to be lively, if opinionated, company, with original views on a variety of subjects and an impressive record of doomed relationships, which he recounts frankly but without apparent rancour. 'Now,' he says, 'I think, underneath, all women are the same. Crazy. Now I get most pleasure from riding my bike.' Zena makes no mention of wife or family, although he tells me he is building himself a house – 'une grande maison' – just out of Taravao. He makes a lot of jokes in French, most of which I cannot understand, and laughs at everything Emile says. A gentle, strong, amiable man, Zena would make a very good comrade in a war, it occurs to me.

After the fire dies down, we drag ourselves under the tarpaulin and fall asleep on the muddy ground, where my dreams are accompanied by the relentless roar of the reef waves thirty metres below.

The sandy cove at the bottom of the bank is useful as an ablution facility. A small waterfall tumbles down the lava cliff, making a fine shower, and the rock pools are good for cleaning the teeth in. Next morning, while doing this, I glimpse a movement in the sea just beyond the reef. Scrambling up on to the rocks, I see a pair of cavorting and spouting humpback whales. They're so close I could jump from the rocks and land on their backs, if I were brave enough. I call up to the others and they too come and watch. Zena tells me that 'les baleines' come close to the reef so that they can rub the barnacles off their bodies on the coral. Minutes later the huge creatures wallow their way down the coast and out of sight.

For the next two days the forest clearing becomes our kitchen, lounge and dining room, the beach our bathroom. Zena is remarkable, a blend of Sherpa Tensing, legendary Maori Guide Rangi and chef Robert Carrier. One day he tosses a line from the rocks and catches small reef fish for dinner; the next day he scoops up crevettes – freshwater prawns – from the stream, catching them in his pareu. During the day the three of us make forays further along the spectacular, untamed eastern coast of Tahiti Iti, while Marcel stays behind to guard the camp.

It is not easy hiking territory. The cliffs are steep, the way often blocked by waterfalls and swift-flowing streams. Sometimes we have to climb the cliffs hand over hand, using ropes which Zena has tied to the trunks of trees. It's tough going, swinging from the end of a knotted rope and hauling ourselves up a slippery cliff, with boulders and rushing water waiting below if we slip. One day, following a river into the interior, we come to the foot of a cataract, eighty metres high, that spills down a black rock face in a hundred silken threads, turning it as shiny as patent leather.

Later, making our way further around the coast, we come across the remains of a prehistoric marae, a platform of stone built on a small plain at the foot of the cliffs. Evidently the ancient Tahitians knew this coast well. As we make our way through a pandanus grove on the plain, Emile says, 'I feel I am the first white man to be here.' It's corny, but I share the feeling.

On the second afternoon it rains, without warning and in a grand deluge. Finding shelter under an open-sided shed built and used by the French military, we lunch on tinned fish and discuss corruption in politics. 'We have no corruption in New Zealand politics,' I suggest, 'because our politicians have no imagination.' Emile waves a now-stale baguette at me, and declares in his usual opinionated manner, 'There has been only one incorruptible French leader. Only one.' He looks at me challengingly. 'Guess who?'

At each name I reel off – Napoleon III, Pétain, de Gaulle, Mitterand – he shakes his head. 'All corrupt. In some way, all corrupt.' Then, grinning at the irony, he supplies the answer: 'The one responsible for the reign of terror. *Robespierre*. Murderous, but incorruptible.'

I have to admit, Emile's French lessons are effective. By the end of the hike I can even write a minimalist rhyming poem in his language:

J'ai vu
la boue
partout.

And la boue, the mud of Tahiti Iti, probably because of its origins in volcanic soil, proves hard to erase. Even after scrubbing and later dry-cleaning my sleeping bag, a dark brown stain remains obdurately along one side.

On my return to Papeete, I check in for one night at the de luxe Sheraton Hotel. When I turn up at reception, filthy, feral, unshaven and dishevelled, I expect the staff to take one look and call security. But they are completely unfazed. I sign the register with a mud-encrusted hand, and the Tahitian porter carries my sodden boots and grimy pack to my room. And there, even as I luxuriate in a steaming hot bath and scrub at the mud, my mind is still on the wild side.

THIRTEEN

LOSING ERROL
TAHITI

'I'M GOING ON THE Circle Island Tour. They said a 9.30 a.m. pick-up. It's late.' The man sitting opposite me in the hotel lobby in downtown Papeete clutches a plastic disposable camera. He's about fifty, thickset, balding, with a flushed flat face, thin lips and gold-rimmed spectacles. His accent is English, with an overlay of New Zealand.

'It's only 9.35 now,' I point out.

'Are you going on the Circle Island Tour too?'

'Yes.'

He gets up and extends his hand. 'I'm Errol. From Morrinsville. I'm a schoolteacher. Primary school. Nine-year-olds, mainly.'

His anxious, florid face and pudgy body remind me of Billy Bunter. He wears a bright purple shirt covered in yellow tropical flowers and the names of the Hawaiian islands. His trousers are dark blue, his black shoes heavy, so that his top half is in the tropics, his lower half still in Morrinsville. He keeps glancing around, through the open doorway, at busy

Boulevard Pomare. A thin, barefooted Tahitian woman is hosing down the tiled pavement, which was covered with the dust which regularly coats everything in Papeete. Behind Errol a white minibus with *Tahiti Tours* on its side draws up.

'Here it is,' I tell Errol, and he scrambles to his feet.

The driver introduces himself as Teva. He's in his late twenties, part-Tahitian, part-Rarotongan, a slim, handsome man with glossy, raven-black hair. The only other passenger is a middle-aged Chilean woman who sits up at the front next to Teva, casting admiring glances at him as he drives out of town. She is dark and plump, with buck teeth, and is dressed in a tight white T-shirt and crimson trousers. She looks at the light rain that is falling and says to Teva reproachfully, 'I leave the sun in Chile to come to Tahiti, and I get rain. I fly all night, twelve hours, and here it rains.'

Teva smiles patiently. 'It's just a shower, it won't last. For the last few weeks here, fine weather every day.'

Errol leans forward. 'It's been dry at home, too. No rain in Canterbury for ages. Or Marlborough. Things are getting desperate.'

The Chilean woman stares at him, mystified by the place-names.

'Our wet season is from November to March.' Teva is speaking into a hand-held microphone now. 'Right now, the dry season.'

'It's dry now in Fiji, too,' says Errol. 'And Samoa. Dry all over the Pacific at this time of the year.'

I'm sitting a couple of rows behind Errol. Although the front half of his head is bald, the rear half is covered in wispy black hair which grows in rows right down his wide flat head and inside his Hawaiian shirt collar.

We drive eastwards, through the sprawling suburbs of Papeete and out of the town. The road hugs the coast. On this eastern side of the island there's only a narrow coastal plain; to our right, lava cliffs rise sheer from the road. Teva points out some springs which burst from the foot of the cliffs, and near Papenoo we see women filling plastic water bottles from pipes jammed into the basalt rock.

This is Tahiti's windward shore, and the reef is intermittent and close in. The freshwater streams which pour down from the mountains prevent any continuous coral formations from occurring here, and the easterly trade winds batter the coast, bringing rain which saturates the slopes and often causes landslides. But today, now that the shower has passed, the sky is clear and burning blue. Past Papenoo, Teva stops and points out scores of young people bobbing in the bay below the road. The waves are sloppy but there are plenty of them. Teva takes up his microphone again.

'Surfing is very popular in Tahiti. We have a stage of the world championships held here every year, at Teahupoo.' Two nut-brown surfers scramble up the bank below the road with short boards under their arms. 'Children start with boogie boards, which are cheap, then later they buy proper boards, which are expensive. Some drop out of school and surf all day, every day.'

Errol cranes forward. 'It's the same in the Waikato. The young ones go to Raglan, stay there for weeks, surf all the time. Some of them never go back to school.'

A few minutes later we reach Arahoho, a pretty cove with a black-sand beach and a wave break on a point composed of a lava flow. A surfer lies on top of his board, waiting for the right wave. Teva leads us to a hole about a metre across at the base of the cliff on the landward side of the road. 'Stand here for a minute,' he says. We watch the hole curiously. Without warning, there is a horrendous sucking sound, and a powerful gust of warm air shoots up from the hole, battering our faces. Errol staggers back, clutching his spectacles; the Chilean woman's cigarette is nearly torn from her hand. Teva laughs. 'It comes up from the sea, up a tunnel under the road. A blow-hole. In French, un trou du souffleur.'

Errol adjusts his glasses. 'Just like in Tonga,' he says. 'Blow-holes all along the coast in Tongatapu. The south coast, that is. None on the north coast.'

The coastal plain gradually widens and we pass through the village of Tiare which, in keeping with its name, 'Flower', has won the competition for the prettiest and tidiest in all Tahiti. The road here is bordered with bright lilies; the hedges flare with hibiscus blooms; the village houses are smothered in palms, breadfruit trees, torch ginger and gardenia bushes. The road rises and falls, giving us constantly changing views of the green mountain massif, the crystal-clear waters of the rivers which flow down from it, and the intensely blue Pacific to our left. This is a wild, unspoilt, picturesque coast. The beach sand is black, but I'm not bothered by that. I grew up beside the sea in Taranaki, where the sand was never any other colour.

Teva describes the flora of the island. 'We have hundreds of introduced plant species in Tahiti. Trees, shrubs, flowers.

Many were brought early last century by an American botanist, Harrison Smith. He started the famous botanical gardens at Papeari.'

'Was that the same Harrison Smith who built hydro-electric power stations in New Zealand? In the South Island?' asks Errol.

Teva frowns. 'I don't think so. No, it can't be. This Harrison Smith was a botanist.'

He guides the bus unhurriedly around the headlands. We pass a group of Tahitians preparing to launch their pirogue, an outrigger canoe. Teva comments into his microphone: 'Unemployment is quite high in Tahiti, but many people who don't have a regular job get by, fishing for mackerel and bonito or growing their own food.'

'It's like that in Rarotonga,' says Errol. 'Catch their own fish, grow their own food. Self-sufficient there, too.'

Teva nods, continues his commentary. 'But many people have come to Tahiti from the outer islands, from the Tuamotus, from the Marquesas. They put a lot of pressure on resources.'

'Just like the Cook Islands,' Errol says. 'People come to Rarotonga from the outer islands, take a lot of land, a lot of fish from the lagoon.'

The Circle Island Tour reaches its quarter mark at Hitiaa, adjacent to the anchorage of French voyager Louis-Antoine de Bougainville, whose frigate appeared on the horizon here in 1768. He was the second European explorer after Samuel Wallis to arrive in Tahiti. With some difficulty Bougainville's ship managed to enter the lagoon at Hitiaa, then stayed for nine days. On his return to France his vivid descriptions of Tahiti were published, and delighted French readers. A plaque commemorating Bougainville's visit has been placed beside the road at Hitiaa, and adorned with an apricot-coloured bougainvillea.

We get out of the bus and look at a river which flows, shallow and translucent, into the sea. Teva points to a coconut palm draped with a climbing plant: 'Fruit salad plant. It lives off the coconut palm, see?'

'Epiphyte,' adds Errol quickly. 'Very common in Sri Lanka, that genus.'

For one wild moment I consider shoving him over the bridge rail and into the river. Errol is not just a bore, he's a *super*bore, a *titanic* bore. I don't know why he bothered to come on this tour – he already knows everything, has seen everything and been everywhere. He pesters and browbeats poor Teva at every opportunity. Teva is admirably patient, clearly used to dealing with tedious tourists, but I can't stand it for much longer. Errol's pudgy face and incessant drone have become anathema. And the worst part is, we're only a quarter of the way around the island. I will have to endure his company for another five hours, until the circle's complete and I get to Taravao, where I'm booked to stay the night. *Five more hours of Errol.*

The coastal plain widens ('Just like the eastern side of Vanua Levu. That's in Fiji'). Partly to control my hands, which are twitching with the urge to garrotte Errol, I pick up the map Teva has given us, and see that we're now in the district of Faaone, approaching Taravao and the isthmus that joins the two islands, Tahiti Nui and Tahiti Iti. Teva points to a grove of mature but unusually stunted coconut palms: 'Those are especially bred so that their crowns grow low to the ground, to make it easier to harvest the nuts.'

Right on cue, Errol comes in. 'Yes, that species was developed in Queensland. They have them in the Philippines, too.'

At that moment, still staring at the map in my hand, and trying unsuccessfully to block out the sight and sound of the hideous Morrinsvillian, I have a flash of inspiration. Obviously, Errol won't leave me; ergo, I must leave Errol. Why not get Teva to drop me off *now*, in Taravao? It'll mean arriving a few hours early at my hotel but give me more time on the isthmus. And, as Teva's tour goes daily, I could arrange to get picked up tomorrow during his next circuit and finish the tour *sans Errol*.

I move up to the front of the bus, out of earshot of Errol, and let Teva know my plan.

'No problem,' he says, looking at his watch. 'Hotel Fare Nana'o is just up here. I'll see you out on the road there, midday tomorrow.'

As I stand on the side of the road with my bag at my feet, watching the bus depart, I catch a glimpse of Errol's face at the window. Realising that his audience has now been halved, he looks as if he is about to burst into tears.

Bliss. Before me is the sea, beneath me is the sea, around me is the sea. Above me is a roof of woven palm fronds and the Tahitian sky. Fare Nana'o is built on piles set into an islet of coral rock, two steps from the beach. But it's a world away from that overpriced Pacific cliché, the 'overwater bungalow'. Its creators, Jean-Claude and Monique Meriaux, were Parisians who wanted to lead a completely new life. Twenty years ago they came to Tahiti and bought a strip of coastal land near Taravao. Jean-Claude was a builder but an unorthodox one. Relishing the availability of the natural tropical materials, he began constructing by hand a house for him and Monique and their eight children.

When the large, low house was completed, he decorated it with his big wooden sculptures, then built a fare – a thatched hut – among the rampant foliage. He used peeled logs, drift-wood, rough-sawn timber and palm fronds, and gave the fare a steeply pitched roof. Then he built another, beside the sea, out of the same materials. When a storm blew over an ironwood tree on the property, so that its big trunk leaned out over the lagoon, Jean-Claude sawed off its branches and built a fare in its crown, like an eagle's nest – a very comfortable eagle's nest, with beds, tables and a small library, reached by climbing along the leaning trunk by a series of notches cut into it. Jean-Claude and Monique called their unique tree house Fare Aito, and their tree-engulfed complex Fare Nana'o.

My fare – Fare Heremeti – is a little way along from the tree house. It has a table built around a centre post, well-stocked bookshelves with reading matter in French and English, an attic bed reached by a driftwood ladder and, from its deck, a hypnotic view of Taravao Bay and the slopes of Tahiti Iti. When I crumble the leftover bits of a baguette and drop them from the deck, they're gobbled up by the reef fish which glide and dart among the coral formations below.

Some years ago, Jean-Claude and Monique separated, leaving Monique to run Fare Nana'o. She is a serene, kind, sophisticated woman, a history graduate of the Sorbonne and a survivor of the student revolution of the 1960s. Meals are taken communally at the main house, in a slate-floored dining room whose walls are an interesting jumble of bookshelves, original paintings and wooden sculptures. At lunch I sit between Tuco, an Easter Islander who is a gardener at the hotel, and Bertha, a Tahitian girl who helps in the kitchen. Lunch is baked mackerel, netted this morning in the lagoon, poisson cru and salad, with wine from Bordeaux. Conversation is in Franglais. Everything is done without fuss or formality, and, best of all, it's Errol-free.

When Monique learns that I prefer to explore by bike, she finds one for me. I cycle around the edge of the lagoon, past the little boat harbour and up a hill into Taravao village, which stretches like a belt around the narrow waist of the isthmus. The last section of the road is steep, and as I push the bike up the short hill I see that I am being watched by a young, heavily armed French soldier standing behind the barbed-wire gate of the military barracks which forms the core of Taravao.

For hundreds of years this two-kilometre-wide isthmus has been of crucial strategic significance. Before European colonisation it was a vital portage for canoes, and so fiercely contested territory for the warring tribes on both islands. In 1844 the French built a fort on the isthmus to subdue the Tahitians, who thought foreign rule an unappealing prospect, and there have been French troops here ever since.

I park my bike outside the big supermarket in the centre of Taravao, and go inside to buy a bottle of water and a baguette. At the checkout are clusters of soldiers, very young men in tight-fitting, mud-brown shirts, shorts and combat boots. Their shorts in particular look impossibly tight. Big, athletic and tanned, with closely cropped hair, the soldiers look like boy scouts on steroids. Then, amid the babble of French, I hear a loud American voice: 'Okay, guys, move along there will yuh?' It comes from a tall, angular soldier in his mid-twenties.

'You're from the *United States* Army?' I ask in surprise.

He points to the yellow-lettered regimental patch on his army shirt pocket. 'Yessir! US Marines!'

'But what are you doing here?'

'Whirr here fur cross-training. Month of cross-training with the French. You a Britisher?'

'No, I'm from New Zealand.'

'That so? I was in Sydney last year.'

'Cross-training?'

'You got it.' He turns away. 'Okay guys, let's get our asses back to barracks.'

The road to the plateau of Taravao climbs straight and steady up the slopes of Tahiti Iti. My bike is well geared and takes the slope without exhausting its rider. What surprises me is that the land here is mostly in pasture: lush green grass grazed by some strange breed of dairy cow with a rust-coloured hide. Standing tall among the pastures are groves of trees, mostly mangoes and eucalypts, and the fields are enclosed by hedgerows. The grazing herds, rich pastures and hedgerows look just like parts of Normandy, until I glance at the wavy coastline far below. Not many coconut palms in Normandy.

From the 750-metre plateau the view is panoramic. The western sweep of Tahiti's sloping, tree-studded pastureland tapers as it descends to the narrow isthmus, then broadens and rears up abruptly to the multiple Matterhorns of Tahiti Nui, forest-covered, precipitous, misty. From up here the sheltered western coast of both islands is laid out far below, a suture line of reef, currents like stretch marks, and two broad breaches in the reef where surfers zigzag among the wave breaks like water-bugs. Relishing what must be one of the loveliest views in the South Pacific, I reluctantly mount my bike and begin the long freewheeling ride back to Taravao, the soft wind cooling my face, pushing back my hair.

It's hard to pull myself away from Fare Nana'o. It's tranquil, natural and beautiful – no overpriced boutiques, no fancy cocktails, no pressure to take part in banal activities – and the only sound is the soughing of the sea under the floorboards. But I have to move on. There is the Circle Island Tour to complete.

Monique rings Tahiti Tours and confirms that Teva will be coming past at noon. I share a last coffee with Tuco, Bertha and the others, then carry my case out to the roadside and sit under a breadfruit tree to await the arrival of Teva's minibus. As I admire the green cone of Tahiti Iti, the bus hoves into view and draws up alongside me. Teva greets me affably and I pull open the bus's side door. As it slides back I hear a voice, a loud voice, a voice I know. 'Hello again! You take the high road and I'll take the low road!' *Errol*!

All that's changed is his shirt – he's swapped the purple Hawaiian one for a yellow Hawaiian one. He fixes me with his hideous gaze. 'I enjoyed yesterday's tour so much, I thought I'd do it all over again,' he says, and waves his disposable camera. 'In case there was anything I missed.'

Today, Teva's bus is nearly full, mainly with elderly tourists, most of whom are already half asleep. I find myself a seat near the back, as far away from Errol as I can get. The bus crosses the isthmus and comes to a large inlet. Teva speaks into his microphone: 'This is Papeari. Those wooden stakes and fences you can see there in the bay are mussel farms.'

From the middle of the bus, a voice begins to bray. 'Like in the Marlborough Sounds. They grow mussels like that there, too. On ropes. Just like those ones. Green-lipped mussels.'

FOURTEEN

THE POPULATION SURVEY
TAHITI

BACK IN TAHITI to do more research on the life and times of Paul Gauguin, I'm assigned to meet a man called Jules. I know nothing about him; I don't know where he lives or what he looks like. Waiting somewhat anxiously as various vehicles draw up outside my Papeete hotel, I scan them all for a Jules who's looking for a Graeme. Then, a few minutes after the appointed time, a silver Peugeot 307 draws up on the forecourt and a middle-aged man heaves himself out from behind the wheel. He wears shorts, a ming-blue tropical shirt and baggy navy-blue shorts.

'M'sieur Graeme?'

'Oui. Jules?'

'Yes.'

'Enchantez, M'sieur.'

'Pleased to meet you, too.'

Jules is a large man. A very large man. Not in height – he's shorter than I am – but in girth. He has the build of a Bulgarian wrestler. He also has large ears, a scrubby little moustache, and a head as big, round and hairless as a Moeraki boulder. As we drive out of Papeete towards the east coast of Tahiti, he provides me with the condensed version of his life. Jules has been many things: a translator, a union delegate, an industrial mediator, a teacher and an installer of tinted windows in automobiles. At the moment he drives the school bus on Moorea and guides people like me around Tahiti.

Jules also tells me he was brought up a Mormon but has abandoned that faith, although he still does not drink or smoke. His accent retains traces of his early years in New Mexico with his parents, so that as well as speaking English fluently – his conversation is sprinkled with words like 'para-doxically', 'discerning' and 'sophisticated'– he does so with a Speedy Gonzales accent. He speaks French and Tahitian with equal facility, along with a little German, as befits a man whose bloodlines are European and Polynesian. His English grandfather emigrated to the Marquesas in the 1890s and became a trader on the island of Hiva Oa, where he married a local woman and got to know Paul Gauguin.

Jules is a fountain of knowledge about French Polynesia. I've never met anyone who knows so much about the history of the place, and about who's currently doing what to whom and for how big a rake-off. It's a reminder that Tahiti is really one big village where everyone monitors everyone else's fortunes extremely closely. But there's nothing malicious about Jules: all the gossip he passes on to me is harmless enough – and undeniably interesting. Married for more than thirty years to a Chinese woman with whom he has three adult children, Jules has recently divorced her in favour of a twenty-two-year-old woman 'younger than my daughter'. 'My honey', as he refers to her, was one of his students in Papeete. Jules sighs contentedly. 'And now,' he muses dreamily, 'life is very good again.'

Jules drives us down the wild east coast of Tahiti, where the sea is rough and driven hard on to the rocky shore by south-easterly trade winds, then turns off the coast road and up a valley. 'You been here before?' he inquires.

I peer around. 'No, never.'

'This is the Faarumai valley,' Jules announces. He slows the car to a crawl along the narrow road. 'A very lovely place.'

Enclosed by walls of volcanic rock, the valley floor is covered with plantation crops: taro, bananas, breadfruit, beans and tomatoes. It is a real-life Garden of Eden. Spread among the trees are small bungalows and lean-tos surrounded by fruit trees and vegetable gardens which seem to burst from the rich, dark soil. About five kilometres long, it tapers to its end at a parapet of sheer rock hundreds of metres high, down which three separate waterfalls cascade into a large shiny pool. Through the waterfalls' gossamer mist a rainbow appears, its colours shimmering in the still air. Surrounding the pool is dense forest, through which a walkway and a viewing platform have been built. Standing on the platform, I peer up into the mist. High above the valley head, the river which feeds the waterfalls spills over a cleft in the rock.

'Beautiful place, uh?'

'It's lovely, yes.'

'I'm glad you like it.' Jules rubs his great belly. 'Now, I'll tell you a story about the people who live here ...'

When, a few years ago, the territorial government of French Polynesia commissioned a population survey of the region, they found that the birth rate – previously so high it was thought to be well-nigh unsustainable – was at last beginning to decline throughout the islands. There was only one exception – the Faarumai valley. In this secluded place couples were still having seven, eight or nine children per family. At first the demographers were mystified. However, closer investigation revealed that the valley, being narrow and enclosed by perpendicular cliffs, was the only area in French Polynesia which could not receive the region's otherwise comprehensive television service.

'There was nothing else for the people to do in the evenings except fuck,' Jules explains. 'They were careless about contraception, so the women were always pregnant. So, to get the birth rate down, the government arranged for a TV transmitter to be brought in by helicopter and placed right up there.' He points to the lip of the cliff, high above us, where the waterfalls originate. 'Then, a year after TV came to the valley, they did another population survey.'

'And the birth rate had gone down?'

'Uh-uh. The birth rate in the valley had gone up even more.' At my perplexed look, he explains. 'The people were watching the French porn channel on TV every night, getting aroused, then fucking each other even more. So the population grew even faster.' Jules scratches his bald dome vigorously. 'So the Catholic Church entered the picture. Disgusted by all the porn the people were watching, the bishop in Papeete insisted that a special coder be put on the

Faarumai TV signal, so the porn channel was blocked out.'

'And that did the trick, right?'

Jules winces. '*Wrong*. The kids – you know, the teenagers – they easily worked out how to decode the TV signal. So, while their parents were still working in the plantations, they came home from school, went to each other's houses, watched the porn channel, got the hots and started fucking like crazy. So the teenage birth rate rocketed up.' Jules turns away and chuckles. 'Human nature's funny sometimes, eh?'

'It certainly is.' Looking around at the abundant gardens, and the little houses, all now with a TV dish atop their roofs, and imagining the indoor lives of the valley's horny inhabitants, I ask Jules, 'So, what's the latest on the birth rate here?'

Jules chuckles. 'The new figures are due from the Statistics Department next month. The whole of Tahiti is waiting to see.'

We're both still laughing when Jules reaches the beginning of the valley and turns the car back on to the coast road. I have never seen the northern coast of Tahiti Iti, so I ask him to drive me across the Taravao isthmus to the end of the road, to the last village, Tautira. As he does so, Jules tells me that there are government plans to build a second port for the territory out here, because Papeete harbour is now so congested. 'It'll be huge, one that'll take big container ships. And big port facilities, cranes, breakwaters, the works.'

Looking around at the tranquil coast, where there are now just a few fishing boats moored in a tiny harbour, I say, 'But that'll ruin the whole area. And cost a fortune.'

Jules nods sadly. 'Sure. Already the locals are gearing up to fight it. And it's going to mean raising *billions* of francs.'

'Where's that sort of money going to come from?'

'From Paris. From Gaston Flosse's buddy. Jacques Chirac.'

Tautira's an attractive settlement, built right across a level coastal plain, with many new houses on the edge of the lagoon. Although it's tranquil now, it's been blasted by cyclones in recent years, with many houses demolished by wind and waves. The only building that survived the cyclones was the sturdy Catholic church, standing inland near the centre of the plain.

We drive through the village and out the other side, still following the coast closely. Gradually the road gets narrower as it shadows the lagoon edge. Jules keeps up his nonchalant socio-political commentary. 'That guy there' – he points to a tall man dressed only in shorts, who's tinkering with an outboard motor – 'just got out of prison. He was a contractor for the first harbour development. Turns out he embezzled millions of government francs. They gave him four years. He served three, and while he was in there his two sons did exactly the same. Put most of the harbour development money into their own bank accounts. How dumb. You'd think they'd think of something more original, wouldn't you?'

'You would. So what happened to them?'

'They're in prison too. They each got eight years.'

Now the road stops, although there's a track which leads around the island and eventually to Teahupoo. Although we can't go any further, I get out, stand at the mouth of the Vaitepiha River and stare out across the shot-silk sea. It was out there in Vaitepiha Bay, on 8 August 1773, that James Cook anchored his sloop *Resolution* inside the reef. The place is still marked on most local maps of Tahiti as 'Mouillage de Cook', Cook's Anchorage. Cook dropped anchor because he was in a hurry. Scurvy had broken out aboard *Resolution*'s sister ship, *Adventure*, on the way from New Zealand; the crew was in desperate need of fresh fruit and vegetables and he couldn't expend more time getting to Matavai Bay, his favourite anchorage, on Tahiti Nui's north coast. But during the night *Resolution*'s anchor dragged and she almost went on to the reef – she was eventually pulled clear by the longboats of both sloops. While this crisis was occupying the ships' crews, the Tahitians swarmed aboard in a frenzy to trade anything the Europeans wanted for western goods.

'Especially nails?' I remark to Jules.

'Yes, yes. Those Tahitian girls would do anything for a nail.' He grins. 'When I was a young man and read that, I went down to the waterfront with some nails and waved them about. It didn't work. The girls were only interested in dollars.'

Cook sailed away from Vaitepiha Bay shortly afterwards, to his accustomed anchorage at Matavai Bay, but he was here long enough to give this district historical provenance. Driving back along the road, Jules says, 'The Spanish were here too, you know.'

'In Tautira?'

'Yes.'

Sure enough, on the door of the church in Tautira there's a plaque commemorating the 1774 visit of two Spanish ships, a reminder that the Spaniards were among the first European explorers to penetrate the South Pacific. At Tautira the Spaniards built a fort, erected a cross and claimed Tahiti for the King of Spain. Two priests from Lima were left behind. They lived in a house from which they hardly emerged and went home as soon as another Spanish ship called. When Cook returned to the district on his third voyage, in August 1777, again to obtain much-needed fresh food and water, he was affronted by the news that the Spanish had put in a claim for Tahiti. By now regarding both Tahiti Nui and Tahiti Iti as integral parts of Britain, Cook insisted that the Spaniards' cross be removed and replaced with his own. On it he had one of his carpenters carve the subtle rejoinder, 'Georgius tertius Rex Annis 1767, 1769, 1773, 1774 & 1777'. England 5, Spain 1.

FIFTEEN

A MYSTERIOUS HEART
TAHITI

'**W**E ... ANCHORED IN nine fathoms of water, within half a mile of the shore. The land appeared as uneven as a piece of crumpled paper, being divided irregularly into hills and valleys; but a beautiful verdure covered both, even to the tops of the highest peaks.'

So wrote Sydney Parkinson aboard James Cook's *Endeavour*, in Matavai Bay, Tahiti, on 13 April 1769. Parkinson was a twenty-two-year-old artist from Edinburgh, a Quaker and a brilliant botanical illustrator. While he busied himself drawing the myriad plants of Tahiti, his shipmates fell under the spell of the island's women. The *Endeavour* was the third European ship to arrive at Tahiti, following Samuel Wallis's *Dolphin* in 1767 and Louis-Antoine de Bougainville's *Boudeusee* in 1768, so already the Tahitians were well aware of what the crews on the European sailing ships were seeking.

Cook's men must have thought they had arrived in paradise without the inconvenience of dying. The Tahitians had no inhibitions about sex, and any constraints the English-men might have harboured quickly disappeared. The com-monest price for sex, a nail, proved mutually satisfactory, until the supply of nails dwindled and the very structure of the *Endeavour* was threatened.

In downtown Papeete at nine in the morning, late-model Citroens, Peugeots and Renaults are zipping along the four-lane waterfront carriageway, Boulevard Pomare. Some-where in the distance a klaxon wails. A smell of fresh coffee, croissants, jasmine and tiare Tahiti – the fragrant national flower – is in the air. Tethered to the doorstep of the town are luxury yachts from all over the world, their masts rocking like metronomes as they sway in the harbour swell. On the pavements, people of all hues mingle and greet each other. Bonjour, bonjour. Ça va? Très bien, merci. Many are families, typically consisting of a French father, a Tahitian, Chinese or mixed-race mother and a pair of beautiful, caramel-skinned children. The 235-year-old love affair between the races goes on.

Already the sun's heat is fierce, the sky a high-gloss blue. Behind Papeete, rising steeply in ridges to verdant, sawtooth mountains whose peaks are wrapped in cloud, is the mysterious core of Tahiti, the 'crumpled paper' of Sydney Parkinson's journal. *La coeur de Tahiti*. It is a heart I have never seen, but have long been curious about. What is in there? Lakes? Rivers? Villages? Nearly all visitors to Tahiti bypass the heart, barely pausing in Papeete before heading straight out to the enticing islands of the Society Group: Moorea, Huahine, Bora Bora. All I know is that in 1791, two years after the mutiny on HMS *Bounty*, six of the mutineers – John Sumner, John Millward, Thomas Burkitt, William Muspratt, Thomas McIntosh and Henry Hillbrant – fled up one of the valleys of Tahiti in an attempt to escape the vengeance of the pursuing Royal Navy, an expedition led by the merciless Captain Edward Edwards of HMS *Pandora*. The six runaways made it into the interior, but the Tahitians, knowing full well on which side their breadfruit was buttered, betrayed them. The mutineers were captured, and returned to the coast and eventually to England to stand trial.

A four-wheel-drive Toyota utility swings into the lay-by on Boulevard Pomare. A tall, mahogany-brown young man jumps out, shakes my hand, grins widely. 'Bonjour M'sieur. Je m'appelle Poken.' He hefts my bag on to the back of the ute. His long hair hangs down his back, and he wears a baseball cap, blue singlet and dark blue shorts. The circular-patterned tattoos of the Marquesas Islands adorn his sinewy arms and legs.

As we swoop through the traffic of downtown Papeete and head out east of the town, Poken tells me that his mother is Marquesan, his father Tahitian. He honks and waves at people everywhere: road workers, gendarmes, taxi drivers, bus drivers. He explains that he is well known through his cultural group performances. He plays guitar, ukelele and drums; has toured Europe, America and Australasia. He also tells me proudly that he has two children: a boy called Teanuanua, which means rainbow, and a girl called Orama, which means shooting star. Poken is also a cross-island guide, one of several who take people like me into the interior of Tahiti.

On the open road now, we speed past Matavai Bay, where Cook anchored and Parkinson wrote of the mountain view, alongside the lagoon, now still and shiny in the morning sun, past outrigger canoes in which fishermen sit idly, past black-sand beaches and surfers pivoting and twisting in the glassy waves, and come to the village of Papenoo. There Poken swings the ute inland.

I see from the map on my knee that the valley of the Papenoo River cuts wide and deep into the centre of Tahiti. It's the dry season, and the river runs gently over stones and between boulders. The road beside it is unsealed, as rocky as the river bed. To our right and left the sides of the valley rise abruptly to sharp, sinuous ridges hundreds of metres high. Bush extends from the valley floor to the skyline. From time to time we come across men operating earthmoving machinery, taming the river with front-end loaders, bulldozers, excavators, making it tractable by digging trenches, laying culverts, and building dams, steel bridges and small hydro-electric power stations. The Papenoo is a source of power and fresh water for the people of coastal Tahiti. Forty percent of the island's electricity comes from hydroelectric schemes.

In the wet season, from November to March, the in-spate river must be formidable, but the going now is surprisingly easy. Poken's ute eases us over bumps and boulders, climbing steadily alongside the watercourse. Studying the map again, I notice a recurring French word I have never seen before. *Gué*. There is a number beside it and the other gués: Gué 4, Gué 5, and so on. 'What is gué?' I ask. Poken twists the wheel to avoid a boulder, tries to explain in his halting English. 'It is ... when ... there is no bridge, but we still must cross. Go *through* the river in the truck.'

'Oh, a ford.'

Poken's frown deepens. 'No. A Toyota.'

'No. Gué, a ford.'

'Toyota.' He points to the vehicle's name on the gear change. Before I'm able to explain, we come to another gué. Here the river is wide and swift, and Poken drives straight into it. The truck becomes a kind of submarine and the water comes up to then over the bonnet. The engine is unaffected. As we emerge on to the shingle on the far side, I say to Poken, 'That was some gué. En Anglais, a *ford.*'

'Ah,' he replies, finally understanding. But he shakes his head in confusion, obviously struck by the irrationality of English. Why name a vehicle after a place in the river that you drive through?

The river flows passively as we continue to climb alongside it. Opposite Gué 5 a waterfall, Cascade Vaiharuru, spills vertically into a pool, its backdrop a wall of bush-covered rock. We pass another hydroelectric station, a tidy modern building built over the river. I'm struck by the total absence of power lines or pylons. The fully automated stations have been designed by French engineers to blend as much as possible with the valley environment. Transmission lines are all underground, so that apart from the small rectangular buildings and the low hum of the turbines within them, the valley is undisturbed by the power-generating developments.

Climbing more steeply, we round a tight bend and pull over to the roadside for a fruit drink and a biscuit. Now I can see the head of the Papenoo valley. It is an enormous basin eight kilometres wide, enclosed by ramparts of rock and serrated peaks, the remnants of a huge volcanic crater which collapsed a million years ago. What strikes me is the scale and steepness of the mountains. One which looks unclimbable lies directly in front of us, blocking the head of the valley like a massive battlement. This is Mt Tetufera, 1,800 metres high and Tahiti's third highest mountain. Tetufera is not a peak but a sheer green wall several kilometres across, its rock face grooved from top to bottom by cascading water. Its summit ridges stand dramatically against the pure blue sky.

'In the wet season,' says Poken, 'many cascades on Tetufera. Very beautiful.' It's not hard to imagine the merging waterfalls forming a silver veil over the face of the mountain.

We pass a larger dam, climb a rough, zigzagging road and emerge on to a flat-topped bluff, on which there's a complex of one-storey buildings. This is Relais de la Maroto, the only inland hotel in Tahiti.

When the hydroelectric schemes began, a place was needed to accommodate the workers so that they could avoid the long, lumpy drive to Papeete and back every day. An accommodation block and dining area were built here, high in the catchment zone. When the dams and powerhouses on the upper reaches of the Papenoo river were completed, the hostel was converted to a hotel. *Relais* is one of those French words which is not quite translatable into English. It means a wayside inn which has a reputation for serving fine food.

The director of Relais de la Maroto is a young Tahitian-born Frenchwoman, Christina Auroy, whose father, Dominique, a

Poken goes off for a smoke
s me the view from the hotel
the relais is built on the edge
we look down to where the
and over basalt boulders, its
mountain-fed water. The air
only noise that of gushing
about the railing like minia-
helicopters, at the front of
few hundred dollars you can
irport up and over the great
drop in for lunch at Maroto.
ook *down* on Tahiti's highest
s high and just over a ridge to
the west of the Papenoo valley.

My room is on the top floor of the dormitory block. Walking along the gallery, I notice that instead of numbers the rooms
have the names of French wines on the door: 'Nuits Saint
Georges', 'Château Lafite Rothschild', 'Châteauneuf du Pape'
and so on. To my disappointment, I'm shown into 'Pétrus'. I've
not heard of Pétrus. I'd rather be next door in 'Château Lafite
Rothschild', which I know is a fine wine. Still, 'Pétrus' is clean,
fresh and comfortable, and from the balcony there's a splendid
view up the valley.

Poken heads off in his truck, after agreeing to pick me up
on his way through later in the week. After a siesta – the sun
is still ferocious – I head up to the bar for a Hinano beer, and
there meet the maitre d'hôtel, Noel. Like the majority of
people on the island, he is part-Tahitian, part-French: in the

local parlance, a *demi*. Noel is an affable young man, in spite of his right hand and lower arm being heavily strapped and bandaged – the result, he tells me, of a fall in the mountains which gashed his wrist.

As we sit and chat, I notice that an unusual number of the men coming and going about the hotel are, like Noel, nursing injuries. Here a bandaged knee, there a strapped ankle; here a patched eye, there a dressed ear. The pharmaceutical business in Tahiti must be booming. When these walking wounded meet, they greet each other with a handshake in the French manner, then refer to each other's injuries, proudly, as if comparing chest sizes. One man with a heavily bandaged leg limps up to Noel, grips his (left) hand, points to Noel's afflicted wrist, then at his own wound, and speculates as to which of them will be more handicapped sexually. Being French, neither man concedes that there is a serious problem. 'It's my hand that's strapped, not my cock,' Noel laughs. As for this propensity to injury, a friend later explains that many Tahitians are reckless to the point of lunacy. They seem to believe they are immortal. Later, back in Papeete, I witness two adults and two children crammed on to a Vespa scooter and weaving through the rush-hour traffic, a barefoot girl on a bike hanging on to the tray of a speeding truck, and helmetless Vespa riders racing three abreast down the motorway.

The Relais de la Maroto remains a watering hole for everyone who works in the mountains. At lunchtime gangs of sweaty men, many wearing bandages, come trooping in for a beer and a meal, mixing readily with the well-dressed visitors who are passing through on a day excursion. As always in French-derived society, meal times are sacrosanct. The tables on the deck are filled with visitors: a mélange of brown-skinned Tahitians, dusky New Caledonians, chic French, slender Chinese, and their offspring, children straight from the melting pot who will grow up without racial prejudice because they carry the genes of three regions – Europe, Asia and Polynesia.

One thing puzzles me about these visitors, though. When they arrive Noel takes them first not to the bar, or the restaurant, or even the toilets. Instead they go off with him down some steps beside Christina's office. When they return about half an hour later, they go out to the deck to dine. After seeing this happen several times, I ask Noel where he takes the guests.

'Oh, à la cave,' he replies.

'La cave?'

'Oui. Would you like to see it?'

We go down three flights of concrete steps to the bottom of the dormitory block. There Noel unlocks a door and switches on a light to reveal a long, cool room whose concrete, windowless walls are lined with wooden shelves filled with bottles of wine. French wine. Very good French wine. At one end of the cellar are tables and chairs, racks of glasses and, on the walls, detailed maps of French wine districts colour-coded with different vintages. Côte de Beaune, Bordeaux, Côtes du Rhône. Noel explains that Christina's father came originally from the Beaune district of the Bourgogne, one of France's leading wine-growing regions. After he arrived he had a cellar built, then shipped over 3,000 bottles of French wine and cellared them here in air-conditioned comfort, at 16 degrees

Celsius. A wine club down in Papeete regularly helicopters up here for tastings; casual visitors to Maroto also call in. So dedicated is Dominique Auroy to cultivating grapes that he's even started a vineyard on Rangiroa atoll, in the middle of the Tuamotu archipelago, 355 kilometres north-west of Tahiti. And, outlandish as it may seem, his three hectares of Carignan grapes, cultivated on a tropical atoll, are now producing fine wines.

As I wander about the cellar, appreciating its coolness and richness, a thought occurs to me. 'Noel,' I ask, 'do you have a wine called Pétrus?'

His expression becomes very respectful. 'Oh yes, we have three bottles of Pétrus.' He leads me to a space where a trio of dusty bottles of red wine lie. 'They are our rarest wine,' he declares, then watches nervously as I pick up one of the bottles. It has an unpretentious, even dowdy label. Later, when I study Le Relais de la Maroto's wine list, I begin to appreciate Noel's discomfort. Pétrus sells for over US$750 a bottle. I am now much happier with my room.

From the balcony of Pétrus I can see, at the head of the valley far below, an area of cleared, level land, surrounded by bush, on which there stand some low, rectangular structures. I consult the map and work out that this must be the 'Site archéologique de Farehape marae'. From boyhood I have harboured a fantasy of being an archaeologist, so I grab my pack and head off down to the valley.

The road is rough, and because of the steepness of the descent it doubles back on itself several times. At the bottom of the valley the heat is overpowering. Parched, leaden-legged, I trudge up the road, and ten minutes later reach the clearing.

The coarse grass shows signs of being recently attacked by a weedeater. Stepping up on to the site of the ancient marae, I see that it is a low platform of blackened, closely fitted river stones. In traditional Tahitian society the marae was the centre of community and ceremonial activities. Here the primary gods, Tane, Tu, Oro and Ta'aroa, were worshipped, and here too a family's lineage was inscribed in stone, delineating its specific rank in the social hierarchy. The marae was also a memorial whose raised stones and posts recalled deceased chiefs and ancestral lines. Here at Farehape, with the bush cleared away, I can see that the several marae are perfectly intact: the platforms of neatly fitting stones, and the rectangular, low-walled enclosures with their upright genealogical markers, stand out starkly in the clearing. A noticeboard informs me that some of the stone stages were platforms where the Tahitian élite carried out their archery contests. Clearly, the Papenoo valley was once an area of vigorous social, religious and sporting activity. But why here, in this remote place? And, if it was such a significant settlement, why did the people abandon it?

I notice signs of human activity at the far end of the terrace. A group of people is doing some sort of work on one of the stone platforms. Strolling down to investigate, I see that most are young Tahitians in shorts and singlets. Young men mainly, but also a couple of young women. They grin and greet me: 'Bonjour M'sieur,' 'Bonjour,' 'Bonjour.'

A square about two metres by two metres and half a metre deep has been cut into the marae floor. Strings have been pegged across the small, neat excavation. In the background a platform of bamboo has been set up. There are plans and notebooks on it. I would love to know exactly what is going on here, but how to ask? My French is not archaeologically refined. Then I notice that one man seems to be directing operations. He is European, tall, athletic, deeply tanned, about thirty, and wearing a long loose mauve singlet, shorts and a back-to-front baseball cap.

'Ah, bonjour M'sieur,' I say as I approach. 'Je m'appelle Graeme. Je suis un écrivain de la Nouvelle Zélande. Q'est-ce que vous faites ici, s'il vous plait?'

His face breaks into a grin, and he extends his hand. 'Hi. I'm Mark Eddowes, from New Zealand. I'm carrying out research here for Otago University.'

It turns out that Mark has been working in French Polynesia for years, excavating archaeological sites from the Marquesas to the Australs. He's fluent in Tahitian and French, has a traditional Tahitian tattoo on one leg, and here in Papenoo is supervising this group of Tahitian archaeology students. He also goes on cruise ships through the islands, lecturing to the passengers on the ethnology of Polynesia, on which he is now a world authority. As we wander over the site Mark explains that this part of the Papenoo valley was once home to thousands of people, as were most of the inland valleys in Tahiti. 'There are hundreds of marae throughout the interior. There's even one on the top of Orohena, the highest peak on the island.'

The valleys' fertile volcanic soils supported crops of taro, sweet potatoes and plantains. The people lived in thatched fares built on stone foundations – paepae – surrounded by the marae. 'Tahitian society was strongly lithic,' Mark goes on. 'This area was a source of stone for tools as well as building. We've been excavating the floors of various fares, and we've found stone implements and the remnants of hearths. It was cooler up here at certain times of the year, so they needed fires for heating as well as cooking, and to keep the mosquitoes away, probably.' The inland valleys remained densely populated until the European missionaries arrived, from 1797 onwards. 'After the Tahitians were converted to Christianity,' Mark tells me, 'the people moved down to the coasts because the churches, mission schools and ports were built there. The interior of the island was largely abandoned.'

Mark is an enthusiast, a personable man who has immersed himself in this reconstruction of Tahiti's pre-European past. I suggest that it's good to see the young people joining in. He agrees: 'Most of them are very good students.' He pauses and shouts a directive to two young men who are erecting a shade tarpaulin over the excavation site. 'The main problem is stopping them smoking dope. Sometimes they go into the bush to cut a pole, and they come back so stoned they forget what the pole was for.' Marijuana growing and smoking is rife in Tahiti.

On the way back, burning with the midday heat, I pause at a place where twin rivulets pour down between boulders into a small, deep pool. I strip off and slip into the mountain water. It is wonderfully cool, clean, revitalising. Opening my eyes under water, I swim up to where it pours, foaming and bubbling, between the boulders. It is like swimming in champagne. Vintage champagne.

In the evening I dine alone in the plush dining room of the relais. It's half dark and eerily silent. The young Tahitian waitress serves me the entrée, then vanishes. The prawn terrine, smothered in a rich, brown Roquefort sauce, is a minor work of art. Its pièce de résistance is the front end of the shell of a small crayfish, presumably the former owner of the curved tail which crowns the terrine. The carapace is about three centimetres long, a beautifully moulded, smooth, ginger-brown shell. It has a long, flat snout, a pair of very long, severally jointed front legs with elongated pincers, long thin whiskers and a cluster of secondary legs under its body. Its on-stalks eyes seem to express astonishment at finding itself on my plate. The whole complicated arrangement of legs, eyes, feelers and claws reminds me of a Swiss Army knife with all its bits and pieces extended. It is a freshwater prawn – une crevette.

When Noel calls into the dining room I express admiration for the crevette's beauty and flavour. He tells me that the creatures live in the river and that Michel, one of the workers, caught this one last night. Then Noel has an idea. 'Would you like to go to catch some crevettes tonight with the chef, Christian?' *Mais oui.*

Michel is a huge Tahitian with a bald head like a cannonball and a gentle, considerate manner. He lends me the pic – the many-barbed bamboo spear – he uses to spear the prawns. Last night, he says, he speared a whole bagful. The chef, Christian, lends me a torch, and the pair of us head off down the steep, rocky road to the river.

Christian is about twenty-five. He comes from Strasbourg and likes living in the mountains because of the tranquillity and the outdoor life. 'No cars, no noise. The only sound here is the river.' At the bottom of the hill we come to the river. Although the moon is full and the sky is light, at ground level it is dark. The river bed is filled with the shadowy shapes of boulders and the sheen of moonlit pools.

Christian explains the technique. We shine our torches into the rock pools. When we spot a crevette we hold the spear over him and, still shining the torch, bring it down on his body, skewering him. It sounds simple, and already I can see a large crevette in a pool, his eyes turned fluorescent red by the torchlight. I hold the spear over him, aim, plunge it down on the prawn. Supposedly. In fact my spear strikes only the stone over which the creature was recently hovering. Sweeping the pool with my torch, I can now see no sign of my quarry.

Moving upstream, I illuminate another pool, locate another crevette. Shine, aim, strike. Miss. Two—nil to the crevettes. The problem is that the little crustaceans, with those swivelling eyeballs on stalks, are sharp-eyed and very, very quick. They dart, in reverse, at top speed. Then they vanish. I can see Christian's torch waving about downriver and hear him splashing about. I stumble over to the pool where he is hunting. He has just one crevette in his bag. He suggests we try further downstream. Climbing over boulders, clutching our pics, we scrutinise every pool we come across. The large crevettes seem to have vanished completely. Now there are only tiny ones, who drift about waving their antennae idly. After an hour, hot, tired, wet and frustrated, we give up.

As we take the long, steep road back up to the relais, Christian observes, 'The Tahitians say that when the moon is full, it is no good for catching the crevettes.' It's the empty-handed fisherman's oldest defence – blame the moon. I decide against pointing out that last night, when Michel went crevetting, he caught plenty, and the moon must have been much the same shape as it is now.

Nevertheless, Christian and I look up reproachfully at the gleaming globe. Then I think of the scarpering mutineers from the *Bounty*, who ran away up here to escape their pursuers. Perhaps it was a good thing they were caught. If they hadn't, they would have gone insane trying to catch crevettes. Not that the poor wretches were saved, in any real sense. After being cruelly incarcerated in 'Pandora's Box' – an iron-grilled cell above decks – for weeks on the voyage back to England, and surviving shipwreck on the Barrier Reef off Australia, Burkitt and Millward were tried by the Royal Navy, convicted of mutiny and desertion, and publicly hanged aboard HMS *Brunswick* on 29 October 1792.

Resuming my cross-island journey with Poken the next day, we head off in the direction of Mt Tetufera. Now the road is not really a road, just a grassy track, barely three metres wide, winding tortuously around great bluffs and ridges. To our left is a ravine hundreds of metres deep; ahead is the huge green face of the mountain, so sheer and high it is obvious no road could conquer it. How will we get over Tetufera? I don't dare ask Poken: he is concentrating on keeping the truck on the track, wrestling with the wheel and the gear lever, his face set grimly. Some corners are so tight that we can hardly get around them. The road is still climbing, and although the long grass covering it suggests that it is not used often, I cannot imagine what would happen if we met another vehicle coming the other way. One of us, I suppose, would have to reverse. The very thought makes my palms sweaty.

Now the narrow road is traversing the face of the mountain, past waterfalls and bush-covered bluffs, still with the dizzying drop to our left. I manage a moment of admiration for whoever it was who incised the road into the cliff face, but I'm still bothered by where it will end. We're now well over 1,500 metres high and still climbing. Then, lo and behold, the track swings abruptly right, and we enter a tunnel, about 100 metres long, cut straight through the basalt rock. Grids of reinforcing steel are plastered into its sides and roof, from which water pours constantly. We slosh through and out the other side. 'Very good too-nell, uh?' says Poken. I have to agree. French engineering must be on a par with French cuisine.

On the western side of Tetufera it is all downhill and perilously steep. On several hairpin bends Poken has to reverse and have two shots at cornering. This backside of the mountain is obviously wetter, and on our descent we pass through rain-clouds and stands of tropical forest, huge trees whose boughs and foliage enclose the road. Cataracts spill over the walls of rock to our right, draining away down the mountainside to Vaihiria, Tahiti's largest natural lake.

Gradually, carefully, we follow the river's course down the ravine, through the mountain mist and rain forest to the lower reaches of the valley. Barrages, man-made lakes and small power stations appear once more. Far ahead I can see a patch of blue sky. At last the road levels out as the valley floor widens. There is a house, some coconut and banana palms, plots of taro. Minutes later, more buildings, an expanse of greenhouses, then the valley merges with the coastal plain in the commune of Mataiea, once home to Paul Gauguin, and later to the brilliant young English poet Rupert Brooke. Brooke left England in 1913 after suffering a nervous break-down – the result of a complicated romantic tangle – and spent several months travelling in the South Pacific. He found sanctuary for a time at Mataiea, in the arms of a lovely young Tahitian woman, Taatamata, and, it has been claimed, even fathered a daughter. Lack of funds caused Brooke to depart for England in July 1914; a few months later World War I began, he enlisted, and died of blood poisoning in the Aegean, in 1915.

The sky is wide and blue, the lagoon sparkles in the after-noon sun. Tahiti's interior has been penetrated, its heart explored. As I look back on those huge, green, jagged moun-tains, I think again of awestruck Sydney Parkinson's descrip-tion: 'As uneven as a piece of crumpled paper … a beautiful verdure … even to the highest peaks'. Parkinson was never to see Scotland again. He contracted dysentery in Batavia on the homeward voyage and died on the Indian Ocean, in January 1771. But his marvellous botanical illustrations of Tahiti endure, as does his peerless summation of the physical allure of a high tropical island, an allure which is unending.

Then there is Moorea. Not only artists and explorers, but also writers, scientists and sundry scapegraces have been entranced by the sight of that high volcanic island, Tahiti's neighbour, just a few kilometres away across the Sea of the Moon. It is the first thing that visitors to Papeete notice, and one of the last sights they see as they leave. Moorea is just eight minutes by light plane from Tahiti; twenty minutes by catamaran; forty by car ferry. Any way you go it's a treat. From the air you can stare down at its great saw-tooth peaks, the mottled pink of its lagoon, the white ruffle of its reef waves. Approaching by sea, its green spires seem to rise up from the water, moving slowly and hypnotically into focus.

To appreciate Moorea, however, it's not necessary to go there. It's enough to watch its shifting moods from Papeete. Early in the morning the peaks are a soft, gin-and-tonic blue. By day they are usually concealed by a mosquito net of cloud. In the late afternoon the clouds lift and the sinking sun backlights the island, bringing the mountains into sharp relief. But it is in the early evening that Moorea and the western sky turn on their best show.

Back in my waterfront hotel in Papeete after my traverse of Tahiti, I'm again captivated by Moorea, as no doubt Sydney Parkinson was as he strolled along the black sand of Matavai Bay, sketch-pad in hand. My hotel is not in the prettiest part of Papeete: it's at the eastern end of Boulevard Pomare, the part the locals call the Gaza Strip. By night the streets are full of strutting soldiers and strident music. Raucous vehicles roar past the plump Tahitians hookers who lurk in the shadows of the buildings' colonnades.

The hotel itself is, to put it kindly, unpretentious. Its small lobby contains a few vinyl-covered chairs, some soft drink-

and cigarette-vending machines, and a TV set which is never turned off. The receptionist is a kind young Tahitian woman who gives me a fruit drink every time I change my New Zealand dollars for Polynesian francs because she pities me the exchange rate. Through the tatty curtain behind her sits a morose, chain-smoking, ageing Chinese man with a face as pale as the rind of uncooked pork. The whole building has a sad, soiled, profitless feel about it. Judging by the furtiveness and frequency with which different couples come and go through the little lobby and up the clunky lift, I suspect that some of its rooms rent by the hour. Another curious feature of the hotel is that it has no restaurant or dining room. Finding a place to eat is no problem, however, as every evening over on the waterfront dozens of little food vans — les roulottes — trundle up to dispense everything from crêpes to kebabs. Their braziers glow in the hot black night and the aroma of their dishes invades the waterfront.

On my second-to-last night in Papeete, sitting at a roulotte and looking up from my plate of poisson cru, I notice that my hotel is very high, a fact I had not previously realised. Now I can see that from the top floor there must be a grand view of the harbour and Moorea, a panorama which I long to capture on film.

The next day the sky is almost totally clear, suggesting that sunset conditions will also be favourable. At six o'clock that evening I take the jerking lift and my camera up the four-teenth floor of the hotel. Outside the lift is a small, gloomy landing and a set of bare concrete stairs. At the top of the landing is another landing, covered with dusty, stacked tables and chairs. Behind is a solid door bearing the notice, 'Restaurant Capitaine Cook'. I push past the furniture and try the door. Locked. *Merde*! In minutes the sunset will be starting, and there's no window, no balcony, no view, and thus no photo. Then I notice another stairway to the right of the landing. At the top is another door. I don't hold out much hope of its being open, but climb the stairs anyway and try the door handle. It turns; the door opens.

Before me is a wide, slightly convex expanse of asphalt. There is a concrete shed and a big TV satellite dish, but the roof is otherwise bare. I walk across to its leading edge. It is like standing on the brink of a canyon. There is no guard rail, no guttering, just an updraft of hot tropical air. Far below is Boulevard Pomare, its vehicles as tiny and silent as cars on an architect's model. To my left and right, already pricked by firefly lights, are the buildings of Papeete. Behind them are Parkinson's crumpled paper mountains. But my eyes do not linger on any of these. Instead I stare ahead, over the waterfront, over the Sea of the Moon.

There are only smudges of cloud. As the sun slips below the horizon, the sky begins to flare, suffusing the entire horizon with light, saturating it with variegated colours: red, pink, orange, vermilion. And beneath the sky, looming like a dark iceberg, is the jagged profile of Moorea. It is an opera and I am in the royal box.

Then, with startling speed the colours begin to fade, as if somewhere in the mountains behind me a dimmer switch is being turned. I pick up my camera, frame the scene, pause, and press the shutter.

ACKNOWLEDGEMENTS

Several people have been very generous, not only enabling me to visit the islands of the South Pacific but also providing me with guidance and hospitality while I was there. I would like to thank in particular: in Auckland, Richard Hall, Renae Pocklington, Lola Carter and Robert Thompson; in Rarotonga, Ewan Smith, Mike Mitchell, Brett Porter and Ross Hunter; and in Tahiti, Dany Panero, Taina Meyssonnier, Hina Smith and the late Jack Rowley.

Special thanks, too, must go to artist Andy Leleisi'uao, for the use of his painting 'Lagoon' from his Ufological Village series, on the cover.